Hymns and Spiritual Songs

Isaac Watts

TUTIS Digital Publishing Pvt Ltd

ISBN 978-81-89952-73-0

HYMNS AND SPIRITUAL SONGS

This impression 2007

Published by
TUTIS Digital Publishing Pvt Ltd.
26 Ramasamy Street
T. Nagar, Chennai 600 017

PREFACE

The following extracts from the Doctor's preface contain the substance of his plan in the three different parts into which the Hymns are divided; the whole would have exceeded the limits of a small book.

"Far be it from my thoughts to lay aside the Book of Psalms in public worship; few can pretend so great a value for them as myself: it is the most noble, most devotional and divine collection of poesy; and nothing can be supposed more proper to raise a pious soul to heaven than some parts of that book; never was a piece of experimental divinity so nobly written, and so justly reverenced and admired. But it must be acknowledged still, that there are a thousand lines in it which were not made for a church in our days to assume as its own. There are also many deficiencies of light and glory which our Lord Jesus and his apostles have supplied in the writings of the New Testament: and with this advantage I have composed these Spiritual Songs, which are now presented to the World. Nor is the attempt vainglorious or presuming; for in respect of clear evangelical knowledge, 'The least in the kingdom of heaven is greater than all the Jewish Prophets.' Matt. xi. 11.

"Now let me give a short account of the following composures.

"The greatest part of them are suited to the general state of the gospel, and the most common affairs of Christians: I hope there will be very few found but what may properly be used in a religious assembly, and not one of them but may well be adapted to some seasons either of private or public worship. The most frequent tempers and changes of our spirit, and conditions of our life, are here copied, and the breathings of our piety expressed according to the variety of our passions, our love, our fear, our hope, our desire, our sorrow, our wonder and our joy, as they are refined into devotion, and act under the influence and conduct of the blessed Spirit; all conversing with God the Father 'by the new and living Way' of access to the throne, even the person and the mediation of our Lord Jesus Christ. To him also, even 'to the Lamb that was slain and now lives,' I have addressed many a song; for thus doth the holy Scripture instruct and teach us to worship in the various patterns of Christian psalmody described in the Revelation.

"I have aimed at ease of numbers, and smoothness of sound, and endeavoured to make the sense plain and obvious. If the verse appears so gentle and flowing as to incur the censure of feebleness, I may honestly affirm, that sometimes it cost me labour to make it so.

"In the first part I have borrowed the sense and much of the form of the song from some particular portions of scripture, and have paraphrased most of the doxologies in the New Testament, that contain any thing in them peculiarly evangelical: and many parts of the Old Testament also, that have a reference to the times of the Messiah.

"The second part consists of hymns whose form is mere human composure; but I hope the sense and materials will always appear divine. I might have brought some text or other, and applied it to the margin of every verse, if this method had been as useful as it was easy. If there be any poems in the book that are capable of giving delight to persons of a more refined taste and polite education, perhaps they may be found in this part; but except they lay aside the humour of criticism, and enter into a devout frame, every ode here already despairs of pleasing.

"I have prepared the third part only for the celebration of the Lord's Supper, that, in imitation of our blessed Saviour, we may sing an hymn after we have partaken of the Bread and Wine."

Hymns

Book 1
Collected from the Holy Scriptures

Hymn 1:1.

A new song to the Lamb that was slain.
Rev. 5. 6 8 9 10 12.

1 Behold the glories of the Lamb
Amidst his Father's throne
Prepare new honours for his name,
And songs before unknown.

2 Let elders worship at his feet,
The church adore around,
With vials full of odours sweet,
And harps of sweeter sound.

3 Those are the prayers of the saints,
And these the hymns they raise:
Jesus is kind to our complaints,
He loves to hear our praise.

4 [Eternal Father, who shall look
Into thy secret will?

Who but the Son shall take that book
And open every seal?

5 He shall fulfil thy great decrees,
The Son deserves it well;
Lo, in his hand the sovereign keys
Of heaven, and death, and hell!]

6 Now to the Lamb that once was slain
Be endless blessings paid;
Salvation, glory, joy remain
For ever on thy head.

7 Thou hast redeem'd our souls with
blood,
Hast set the pris'ners free,
Hast made us kings and priests to God,
And we shall reign with thee.

8 The worlds of nature and of grace
Are put beneath thy power;
Then shorten these delaying days,
And bring the promis'd hour.

Hymn 1:2.

The deity and humanity of Christ, John 1. 1-3 14. Col. 9. 16. Eph. 3, 9 10.

1 Ere the blue heavens were stretch'd
  abroad,
From everlasting was the Word;
With God he was; the Word was God,
And must divinely be ador'd.

2 By his own power were all things
  made;
By him supported all things stand;
He is the whole creation's head,
And angels fly at his command.

3 Ere sin was born, or Satan fell,
He led the host of morning stars;
(Thy generation who can tell,
Or count the number of thy years?)

4 But lo, he leaves those heavenly
  forms,
The Word descends and dwells in clay,
That he may hold converse with
  worms,
Dress'd in such feeble flesh as they.

5 Mortals with joy beheld his face,
Th' eternal Father's only Son;
How full of truth! how full of grace!
When thro' his eyes the Godhead
  shone!

6 Archangels leave their high abode
To learn new mysteries here, and tell
The loves of our descending God,
The glories of Imannuel.

Hymn 1:3.

The nativity of Christ, Luke 1. 30 &c.
Luke 2, 10 &c.

1 Behold, the grace appears,
The promise is fulfill'd;
Mary the wondrous virgin bears,
And Jesus is the child.

2 [The Lord, the highest God,
Calls him his only Son;
He bids him rule the lands abroad,
And gives, him David's throne.

3 O'er Jacob shall he reign
With a peculiar sway;
The nations shall his grace obtain,
His kingdom ne'er decay.]

4 To bring the glorious news
A heavenly form appears;

He tells the shepherds of their joys,
And banishes their fears.

5 "Go, humble swains," said he,
"To David's city fly;
"The promis'd infant born to-day,
"Doth in a manger lie.

6 "With looks and heart serene,
"Go visit Christ your King;"
And straight, a flaming troop was
seen;
The shepherds heard them sing:

7 "Glory to God on high,
"And heavenly peace on earth,
"Good-will to men, to angels joy,
"At the Redeemer's birth!"

8 [In worship so divine
Let saints employ their tongues,
With the celestial host we join,
And loud repeat their songs:

9 "Glory to God on high,
"And heavenly peace on earth,
"Good-will to men, to angels joy,
"At our Redeemer's Birth."]

Hymn 1:4.

[Supplement] The inward witness to Christianity, 1 John 5. 10.

1 Questions and doubts be heard no more;
Let Christ and joy be all our theme;
His Spirit seals his gospel sure,
To every soul that trusts in him.

2 Jesus, thy witness speaks within:
The mercy which thy words reveal
Refines the heart from sense and sin,
And stamps its own celestial seal.

3 'Tis God's inimitable hand
That moulds and forms the heart anew;
Blasphemers can no more withstand,
But bow and own thy doctrine true.

4 The guilty wretch that trusts thy blood,
Finds peace and pardon at thy cross;
The sinful soul averse to God,
Believes and loves his Maker's laws.

5 Learning and wit may cease their strife,
When miracles with glory shine;

The voice that calls the dead to life
Must be almighty, and divine.

Hymn 1:5.

Submission to afflictive providences,
Job 1. 21.

1 Naked as from the earth we came,
And crept to life at first,
We to the earth return again,
And mingle with our dust.

2 The dear delights we here enjoy,
And fondly call our own,
Are but short favours borrow'd now,
To be repaid anon.

3 'Tis God that lifts our comforts high,
Or sinks them in the grave;
He gives, and (blessed be his name!)
He takes but what he gave.

4 Peace, all our angry passions, then,
Let each rebellious sigh
Be silent at his sov'reign will,
And every murmur die.

5 If smiling mercy crown our lives,
Its praises shall be spread;
And we'll adore the justice too
That strikes our comforts dead.

Hymn 1:6.

Triumph over death, Job 19. 25-27.

1 Great God, I own thy sentence just
And nature must decay;
I yield my body to the dust
To dwell with fellow-clay.

2 Yet faith may triumph o'er the grave,
And trample on the tombs:
My Jesus, my Redeemer lives,
My God, my Saviour comes.

3 The mighty Conqueror shall appear
High on a royal seat,
And Death, the last of all his foes,
Lie vanquish'd at his feet.

4 Tho' greedy worms devour my skin,
And gnaw my wasting flesh,
When God shall build my bones again,
He clothes them all afresh.

5 Then shall I see thy lovely face
With strong immortal eyes,
And feast upon thy unknown grace
With pleasure and surprise.

Hymn 1:7.

The invitation of the gospel; or, Spiritual food and clothing, Isa. 55. 1 &c.

1 Let every mortal ear attend,
And every heart rejoice,
The trumpet of the gospel sounds
With an inviting voice.

2 Ho, all ye hungry starving souls,
That feed upon the wind,
And vainly strive with earthly toys
To fill an empty mind,

3 Eternal wisdom has prepar'd
A soul reviving feast,
And bids your longing appetites
The rich provision taste.

4 Ho, ye that pant for living streams,
And pine away and die,

Here you may quench your raging thirst
With springs that never dry.

5 Rivers of love and mercy here
In a rich ocean join;
Salvation in abundance flows,
Like floods of milk and wine.

6 [Ye perishing and naked poor,
Who work with mighty pain
To weave a garment of your own
That will not hide your sin,

7 Come naked, and adorn your souls
In robes prepar'd by God,
Wrought by the labours of his Son,
And dy'd in his own blood.]

8 Dear God, the treasures of thy love
Are everlasting mines,
Deep as our helpless miseries are,
And boundless as our sins.

9 The happy gates of gospel grace
Stand open night and day,
Lord, we are come to seek supplies,
And drive our wants away.

Hymn 1:8.

The safety and protection of the church, Isa. 26. 1-6.

1 How honourable is the place
Where we adoring stand,
Zion the glory of the earth,
And beauty of the land!

2 Bulwarks of mighty grace defend
The city where we dwell,
The walls of strong salvation made,
Defy th' assaults of hell.

3 Lift up the everlasting gates,
The doors wide open fling,
Enter, ye nations, that obey
The statutes of our King.

4 Here you shall taste unmingled
joys,
And live in perfect peace,
You that have known Jehovah's name,
And ventur'd on his grace.

5 Trust in the Lord, for ever trust,
And banish all your fears;

Strength in the Lord Jehovah dwells,
Eternal as his years.

6 [What tho' the rebels dwell on high,
His arm shall bring them low,
Low' as the caverns of the grave
Their lofty heads shall bow.]

7 [On Babylon our feet shall tread
In that rejoicing hour,
The ruins of her walls shall spread
A pavement for the poor.]

Hymn 1:9.

The promises of the covenant of grace,
Isa. 55. 1 2. Zech. 13. 1. Mich. 7. 19.
Ezek. 36. 25 &c.

1 In vain we lavish out our lives
To gather empty wind,
The choicest blessings earth can
yield
Will starve a hungry mind.

2 Come and the Lord shall feed our
souls
With more substantial meat,

With such as saints in glory love,
With such as angels eat.

3 Our God will every want supply,
And fill our hearts with peace;
He gives by covenant and by oath
The riches of his grace.

4 Come, and he'll cleanse our spotted souls,
And wash away our stains,
In the dear fountain that his Son
Pour'd from his dying veins.

5 [Our guilt shall vanish all away
Tho' black as hell before;
Our sins shall sink beneath the sea,
And shall be found no more.

6 And lest pollution should o'erspread
Our inward powers again,
His Spirit shall bedew our souls
Like purifying rain.]

7 Our heart, that flinty stubborn thing,
That terrors cannot move,
That fears no threat'nings of his wrath,
Shall be dissolv'd by love;

8 Or he can take the flint away
That would not be refin’d,
And from the treasures of his grace
Bestow a softer mind.

9 There shall his sacred Spirit dwell,
And deep engrave his law,
And every motion of our souls
To swift obedience draw.

10 Thus will he pour salvation down,
And we shall render praise,
We the dear people of his love,
And he our God of grace.

Hymn 1:10.

The blessedness of gospel times; or, The revelation of Christ to Jews and Gentiles, Isa. 5. 2 7-10. Matt.13. 16 17.

1 How beauteous are their feet
Who stand on Zion’s hill!
Who bring salvation on their tongues,
And words of peace reveal!

2 How charming is their voice!
How sweet the tidings are!

"Zion, behold thy Saviour King,
He reigns and triumphs here."

3 How happy are our ears
That hear this joyful sound,
Which kings and prophets waited for,
And sought, but never found!

4 How blessed are our eyes
That see this heavenly light!
Prophets and kings desir'd it long,
But dy'd without the sight.

5 The watchmen join their voice,
And tuneful notes employ;
Jerusalem breaks forth in songs,
And deserts leant the joy.

6 The Lord makes bare his arm
Thro' all the earth abroad
Let every nation now behold
Their Saviour and their God.

Hymn 1:11.

The humble enlightened, and carnal reason humbled; or, The sovereignty of grace, Luke 10. 21 22

1 There was an hour when Christ
rejoic'd,
And spoke his joy in words of
praise;
"Father, I thank thee, mighty God,
"Lord of the earth, and heavens, and
seas.

2 "I thank thy sovereign power and
love,
"That crowns my doctrine with
success;
"And makes the babes in knowledge
learn
"The heights, and breadths, and
lengths of grace.

3 "But all this glory lies conceal'd
"From men of prudence and of wit;
"The prince of darkness blinds their
eyes,
"And their own pride resists the
light.

4 "Father, 'tis thus, because thy will
"Chose and ordain'd it should be so;
"T'is thy delight t' abase the proud,
"And lay the haughty scorner low.

5 "There's none can know the Father right
"But those who learn it from the Son;
"Nor can the Son be well receiv'd,
But where the Father makes him known."

6 Then let our souls adore our God
That deals his graces as he please,
Nor gives to mortals an account
Or of his actions, or decrees.

Hymn 1:12.

Free grace in revealing Christ,
Luke 10. 21.

1 Jesus, the man of constant grief,
A mourner all his days;
His spirit once rejoic'd aloud,
And tun'd his joy to praise.

2 "Father, I thank thy wondrous love,
"That hath reveal'd thy Son
"To men unlearned; and to babes
"Has made thy gospel known.

3 "The mysteries of redeeming grace
"Are hidden from the wise,
"While pride and carnal reasonings join
"To swell and blind their eyes."

4 Thus doth the Lord of heaven and earth
His great decrees fulfil,
And orders all his works of grace
By his own sovereign will.

Hymn 1:13.

The Son of God incarnate; or, The titles and the kingdom of Christ, Isa. 9. 2 6 7.

1 The lands that long in darkness lay
Now have beheld a heavenly light;
Nations that sat in death's cold shade
Are bless'd with beams divinely bright.

2 The virgin's promis'd Son is born,
Behold th' expected Child appear;
What shall his names or titles be?
The Wonderful, the Counsellor.

3 This infant is the mighty God
Come to be suckled and ador'd
Th' eternal Father, Prince of Peace,
The son of David, and his Lord.

4 The government of earth and seas
Upon his shoulders shall be laid
His wide dominions still increase,
And honours to his name be paid.

5 Jesus the holy child shall sit
High on his father David's throne,
Shall crush his foes beneath his
feet,
And reign to ages yet unknown.

Hymn 1:14.

The triumph of faith; or, Christ's unchangeable love, Rom. 8. 33 &c.

1 Who shall the Lord's elect condemn?
'Tis God that justifies their souls,
And mercy like a mighty stream
O'er all their sins divinely rolls.

2 Who shall adjudge the saints to
hell?

'Tis Christ that suffer'd in their
stead,
And the salvation to fulfil,
Behold him rising from the dead.

3 He lives, he lives, and sits above,
For ever interceding there:
Who shall divide us from his love?
Or what should tempt us to despair?

4 Shall persecution, or distress,
Famine, or sword, or nakedness?
He that hath lov'd us bears us thro',
And makes us more than conquerors
too.

5 Faith hath an overcoming power,
It triumphs in the dying hour;
Christ is our life, our joy, our hope,
Nor can we sink with such a prop.

6 Not all that men on earth can do,
Nor powers on high, nor powers
below,
Shall cause his mercy to remove,
Or wean our hearts from Christ our
love.

Hymn 1:15.

Our own weakness, and Christ our strength, 2 Cor. 12. 7 9 10.

1 Let me but hear my Saviour say,
“Strength shall be equal
to thy day,”
Then I rejoice in deep distress,
Leaning on all-sufficient Grace.

2 I glory in infirmity,
That Christ’s own power may rest
on me;
When I am weak, then am I strong,
Grace is my shield, and Christ my
song.

3 I can do all things, or can bear
All sufferings, if my Lord be there;
Sweet pleasures mingle with the
pains,
While his left hand my head
sustains.

4 But if the Lord be once withdrawn,
And we attempt the work alone,

When new temptations spring
and rise
We find how great our weakness is.

5 [So Samson, when his hair was lost,
Met the Philistines to his cost;
Shook his vain limbs with sad
surprise,
Made feeble fight, and lost his
eyes.]

Hymn 1:16.

Hosanna to Christ, Matt. 21. 9. Luke 19. 38 40.

1 Hosanna to the royal Son
Of David's ancient line,
His natures two, his person one,
Mysterious and divine.

2 The root of David here we find,
And offspring is the same;
Eternity and time are join'd
In our Immanuel's name.

3 Bless'd he that comes to wretched men
With peaceful news from heaven;

Hosannas of the highest strain
To Christ the Lord be given.

4 Let mortals ne'er refuse to take
Th' hosanna on their tongues,
Lest rocks and stones should rise,
  and break
Their silence into songs.

Hymn 1:17.

Victory over death, 1 Cor. 15, 55 &c.

1 O for an overcoming faith
To cheer my dying hours,
To triumph o'er the monster Death,
And all his frightful powers.

2 Joyful with all the strength I have
My quivering lips should sing,
"Where is thy boasted victory,
  Grave?
And where the monster's sting?"

3 If sin be pardon'd I'm secure,
Death hath no sting beside;
The law gives sin its damning power,
But Christ, my ransom, died.

4 Now to the God of victory
Immortal thanks be paid,
Who makes us conquerors while
we die,
Thro' Christ our living head.

Hymn 1:18.

Blessed are the dead that die in the Lord, Rev. 14. 13.

1 Hear what the voice from heaven
proclaims,
For all the pious dead,
Sweet is the savour of their names,
And soft their sleeping bed.

2 They die in Jesus, and are bless'd;
How kind their slumbers are!
From sufferings and from sins
releas'd,
And freed from every snare.

3 Far from this world of toil and strife,
They're present with the Lord;
The labours of their mortal life
End in a large reward.

Hymn 1:19.

The song of Simeon; or, Death made desirable, Luke 2. 27 &c.

1 Lord at thy temple we appear,
As happy Simeon came,
And hope to meet our Saviour here;
O make our joys the same!

2 With what divine and vast delight
The good old man was fill'd,
When fondly in his wither'd arms
He clasp'd the holy child!

3 "Now I can leave this world," he cry'd,
"Behold thy servant dies,
"I've seen thy great salvation, Lord,
"And close my peaceful eyes.

4 "This is the light prepar'd to shine
"Upon the Gentile lands,
"Thine Israel's glory, and their hope
"To break their slavish bands."

5 [Jesus, the vision of thy face
Hath overpowering charms

Scarce shall I feel death's cold
embrace
If Christ be in my arms.

6 Then while ye hear my heart-strings
break,
How sweet my minutes roll!
A mortal paleness on my cheek,
And glory in my soul.]

Hymn 1:20.

Spiritual apparel; namely, the robe of righteousness, and garments of salvation, Isa. 61. 10.

1 Awake, my heart, arise, my tongue,
Prepare a tuneful voice,
In God the life of all my joys,
Aloud will I rejoice.

2 'Tis he adorn'd my naked soul,
And made salvation mine,
Upon a poor polluted worm
He makes his graces shine.

3 And lest the shadow of a spot
Should on my soul be found,

He took the robe the Saviour
wrought,
And cast it all around.

4 How far the heavenly robe exceeds
What earthly princes wear!
These ornaments, how bright they
shine!
How white the garments are!

5 The Spirit wrought my faith
and love,
And hope, and every grace;
But Jesus spent his life to work
The robe of righteousness.

6 Strangely, my soul, art thou array'd
By the great sacred Three:
In sweetest harmony of praise
Let all thy powers agree.

Hymn 1:21.

A vision of the kingdom of Christ among men, Rev. 21. 1-4.

1 Lo, what a glorious sight appears
To our believing eyes!

The earth and sea are pass'd away,
And the old rolling skies.

2 From the third heaven where God
resides,
That holy happy place,
The New Jerusalem comes down
Adorn'd with shining grace.

3 Attending angels shout for joy,
And the bright armies sing,
"Mortals, behold the sacred seat
"Of your descending King.

4 "The God of glory down to men
"Removes his blest abode,
"Men the dear objects of his grace,
"And he the loving God.

5 "His own soft hand shall wipe the
tears
"From every weeping eye,
"And pains, and groans, and griefs,
and fears,
"And death itself shall die."

6 How long, dear Saviour, O how
long,
Shall this bright hour delay!

Fly swifter round, ye wheels of time,
And bring the welcome day.

Hymn 1:22. [Supplement.]

Flesh and Spirit. Rom. 8. 1.

1 What vain desires, and passions vain,
Attend this mortal clay!
Oft have they pierc'd my soul with pain,
And drawn my heart astray.

2 How have I wander'd from my God,
And following sin and shame
In this vile world of flesh and blood
Defil'd my nobler frame!

3 For ever blessed be thy grace
That form'd my soul anew,
And made it of an heaven-born race,
Thy glory to pursue.

4 My spirit holds perpetual war,
And wrestles and complains;
But views the happy moment near
That shall dissolve its chains.

5 Cheerful in death I close my eyes,
To part with every lust;
And charge my flesh whene'er it rise
To leave them in the dust.

6 My purer spirit shall not fear
To put this body on:
Its tempting powers no more are
there,
Its lusts and passions gone.

Hymn 1:23. [Supplement.]

A hopeful youth falling short of heaven, Mark 10. 21.

1 Must all the charms of nature then
So hopeless to salvation prove?
Can hell demand, can heaven
condemn
The man whom Jesus deigns to love?

2 The man who sought the ways
of truth,
Paid friends and neighbours all their
due,
(A modest, sober, lovely youth)
And thought he wanted nothing now.

3 But mark the change! thus spake the
Lord,
"Come, part with earth for heaven
to-day,"
The youth astonish'd at the word,
In silent sadness went his way.

4 Poor virtues that he boasted so,
This test unable to endure;
Let Christ, and grace, and glory go
To make his land and money sure.

5 Ah foolish choice of treasures here!
Ah fatal love of tempting gold!
Must this base world be bought so
dear?
Are life and heaven so cheaply
sold?

6 In vain the charms of nature shine,
If this vile passion govern me:
Transform my soul, O love divine,
And make me part with all for thee.

Hymn 1:24.

The rich sinner dying, Psalm 49. 6 9.
Eccl. 8. 8. Job 3. 14 15.

1 In vain the wealthy mortals toil,
And heap their shining dust in vain,
Look down and scorn the humble poor,
And boast their lofty hills of gain.

2 Their golden cordials cannot ease
Their pained hearts or aching heads,
Nor fright nor bribe approaching death
From glittering roofs and downy beds.

3 The lingering, the unwilling soul
The dismal summons must obey,
And bid a long a sad farewell
To the pale lump of lifeless clay.

4 Thence they are huddled to the grave,
Where kings and slaves have equal thrones;
Their bones without distinction lie
Amongst the heap of meaner bones.

The rest referred to Psalm 49.

Hymn 1:25.

A vision of the Lamb, Rev 5. 6-9.

1 All mortal vanities, be gone,
Nor tempt my eyes, nor tire my
ears,
Behold amidst th' eternal throne
A vision of the Lamb appears.

2 [Glory his fleecy robe adorns,
Mark'd with the bloody death he
bore;
Seven are his eyes, and seven his
horns,
To speak his wisdom and his power.

3 Lo, he receives a sealed book
From him that sits upon the throne:
Jesus, my Lord, prevails to look
On dark decrees, and things
unknown.]

4 All the assembling saints around
Fall worshipping before the Lamb,
And in new songs of gospel-sound
Address their honours to his name,

5 The joy, the shout, the harmony
Flies o'er the everlasting hills,
"Worthy art thou alone," they cry,
"To read the book, to loose the
seals."]

6 Our voices join the heavenly strain,
And with transporting pleasure sing,
"Worthy the Lamb that once was
slain,
"To be our teacher and our king!"

7 His words of prophecy reveal
Eternal counsels, deep designs;
His grace and vengeance shall fulfil
The peaceful and the dreadful lines.

8 Thou hast redeem'd our souls from
hell
'With thine invaluable blood;
And wretches that did once rebel
Are now made favourites of
their Cod.

9 Worthy for ever is the Lord,
That died for treasons not his own,
By every tongue to be ador'd,
And dwell upon his Father's throne.

Hymn 1:26.

Hope of heaven by the resurrection of Christ, 1 Peter 1. 3-5.

1 Bless'd be the everlasting God,
The Father of our Lord,
Be his abounding mercy prais'd,
His majesty ador'd.

2 When from the dead he rais'd his
Son,
And call'd him to the sky,
He gave our souls a lively hope
That they should never die.

3 What tho' our inbred sins require
Our flesh to see the dust!
Yet as the Lord our Saviour rose,
So all his followers must.

4 There's an inheritance divine
Reserv'd against that day,
'Tis uncorrupted, undefil'd,
And cannot waste away.

5 Saints by the power of God are kept
Till the salvation come;

We walk by faith as strangers here
Till Christ shall call us home.

Hymn 1:27.

Assurance of heaven; or, A saint prepared to die, 2 Tim. 4. 6 7 8 18.

1 [Death may dissolve my body now,
And bear my spirit home;
Why do my minutes move so slow,
Nor my salvation come?

2 With heavenly weapons I have fought
The battles of the Lord,
Finish'd my course, and kept the faith,
And wait the sure reward.]

3 God has laid up in heaven for me
A crown which cannot fade;
The righteous Judge at that great day
Shall place it on my head.

4 Nor hath the King of grace decreed
This prize for me alone;

But all that love and long to see
Th' appearance of his Son.

5 Jesus the Lord shall guard me safe
From every ill design;
And to his heavenly kingdom keep
This feeble soul of mine.

6 God is my everlasting aid
And hell shall rage in vain;
To him be highest glory paid,
And endless praise.—Amen.

Hymn 1:28.

The triumph of Christ over the enemies of his church, Isa. 63. 1 2 3 &c.

1 What mighty man, or mighty God,
Comes travelling in state,
Along the Idumean road,
Away from Bozrah's gate?

2 The glory of his robes proclaim
'Tis some victorious king:
"'Tis I, the just, th' Almighty One,
"That your salvation bring."

3 "Why, mighty Lord," thy saints enquire,
"Why thine apparel red?
"And all thy vesture stain'd like those
"Who in the wine-press tread?"

4 "I by myself have trod the press,
"And crush'd my foes alone,
"My wrath has struck the rebels dead,
"My fury stamp'd them down.

5 "'Tis Edom's blood that dyes my robes
"With joyful scarlet stains,
"The triumph that my raiment wears
"Sprung from their bleeding veins.

6 "Thus shall the nations be destroy'd
"That dare insult my saints,
"I have an arm t' avenge their wrongs,
"An ear for their complaints."

Hymn 1:29.

The ruin of Antichrist, Isa. 63. 4-7.

1 "I lift my banners," saith the Lord,
"Where Antichrist has stood,

"The city of my gospel-foes
"Shall be a field of blood.

2 "My heart has study'd just revenge,
"And now the day appears,
"The day of my redeem'd is come
"To wipe away their tears.

3 "Quite weary is my patience grown,
"And bids my fury go
"Swift as the lightning it shall move,
"And be as fatal too.

4 "I call for helpers but in vain:
"Then has my gospel none?
"Well, mine own arm has might
enough
"To crush my foes alone.

5 "Slaughter and my devouring sword
"Shall walk the streets around,
"Babel shall reel beneath my stroke,
"And stagger to the ground."

6 Thy honours, O victorious King!
Thine own right-hand shall raise,
While we thy awful vengeance
sing,
And our deliverer praise.

Hymn 1:30.

Prayer for deliverance answered, Isa. 26. 8-12 20 21.

1 In thine own ways, O God of love,
We wait the visits of thy grace,
Our souls desire is to thy Name,
And the remembrance of thy face.

2 My thoughts are searching, Lord, for thee,
'Mongst the black shades of lonesome night;
My earnest cries salute the skies
Before the dawn restore the light.

3 Look, how rebellious men deride
The tender patience of my God;
But they shall see thy lifted hand,
And feel the scourges of thy rod.

4 Hark, the Eternal rends the sky,
A mighty voice before him goes,
A voice of music to his friends,
But threatening thunder to his foes.

5 Come, children, to your Father's arms,
Hide in the chambers of my grace,
Till the fierce storms be overblown,
And my revenging fury cease.

6 My sword shall boast its thousands slain,
And drink the blood of haughty kings,
While heavenly peace around my flock
Stretches its soft and shady wings.

Hymn 1:31. [Supplement.]

The hidden life of a Christian, Col. 3. 3.

1 O happy soul that lives on high;
While men lie grovelling here!
His hopes are fix'd above the sky,
And faith forbids his fear.

2 His conscience knows no secret stings,
While peace and joy combine
To form a life whose holy springs
Are hidden and divine.

3 He waits in secret on his God;
His God in secret sees:
Let earth be all in arms abroad,
He dwells in heavenly peace.

4 His pleasures rise from things unseen,
Beyond this world and time,
Where neither eyes nor ears have
been,
Nor thoughts of sinners climb.

5 He wants no pomp nor royal throne
To raise his figure here;
Content and pleas'd to live unknown,
Till Christ his life appear.

6 He looks to heaven's eternal hill
To meet that glorious day:
But patient waits his Saviour's will
To fetch his soul away.

Hymn 1:32.

Strength from heaven, Isa. 40. 27-30.

1 Whence do our mournful thoughts
arise?
And where's our courage fled?

Has restless sin and raging hell
Struck all our comforts dead?

2 Have we forgot th' almighty Name
That form'd the earth and sea?
And can an all-creating arm
Grow weary or decay?

3 Treasures of everlasting might
In our Jehovah dwell;
He gives the conquest to the weak,
And treads their foes to hell.

4 Mere mortal power shall fade and die,
And youthful vigour cease;
But we that wait upon the Lord
Shall feel our strength increase.

5 The saints shall mount on eagles'
wings
And taste the promis'd bliss,
Till their unwearied feet arrive
Where perfect pleasure is.

Hymn 1:33. [Supplement.]

The gospel the power of God to salvation, Rom. 1. 16. 1 Cor. 1. 18 24.

1 What shall the dying sinner do
That seeks relief for all his woe?
Where shall the guilty conscience
  find
Ease for the torment of the mind?

2 How shall we get our crimes forgiven,
Or form our natures fit for heaven?
Can souls all o'er defil'd with sin
Make their own powers and passions
  clean?

3 In vain we search, in vain we try,
Till Jesus bring his gospel nigh;
'Tis there such power and glory
  dwell
As saves rebellious souls from hell.

4 This is the pillar of our hope
That bears our fainting spirits up;
We read the grace, we trust the word,
And find salvation in the Lord.

5 Let men or angels dig the mines
Where nature's golden treasure
  shines,
Brought near the doctrine of the
  cross
All nature's gold appears but dross.

6 Should vile blasphemers with disdain
Pronounce the truths of Jesus vain,
I'll meet the scandal and the shame,
And sing and triumph in his Name.

Hymn 1:34. [Supplement.]

None excluded from hope, Rom. 1. 16. 1 Cor. 1. 24.

1 Jesus, thy blessings are not few,
Nor is thy gospel weak;
Thy grace can melt the stubborn Jew,
And bow th' aspiring Greek.

2 Wide as the reach of Satan's rage
Doth thy salvation flow;
'Tis not confin'd to sex or age,
The lofty or the low.

3 While grace is offer'd to the prince,
The poor may take their share;
No mortal has a just pretence
To perish in despair.

4 Be wise, ye men of strength and wit,
Nor boast your native powers;

But to his sovereign grace submit,
And glory shall be yours.

5 Come, all ye vilest sinners come,
He'll form your souls anew:
His gospel and his heart have room
For rebels such as you.

6 His doctrine is almighty love;
There's virtue in his Name
To turn the raven to a dove,
The lion to a lamb.

Hymn 1:35. [Supplement.]

Truth, sincerity, &c. Phil. 4. 8.

1 Let those who bear the Christian name
Their holy vows fulfil:
The saints, the followers of the Lamb,
Are men of honour still.

2 True to the solemn oath they take,
Tho' to their hurt they swear;
Constant and just to all they speak,
For God and angels hear.

3 Still with their lips their hearts agree,
Nor flattering words devise,
They know the God of truth can see
Thro' every false disguise.

4 They hate th' appearance of a lie
In all the shapes it wears;
They live the truth; and, when they die,
Eternal life is theirs.

5 While hypocrites and liars fly
Before the Judge's frown,
His faithful friends, who fear a lie,
Receive th' immortal crown.

Hymn 1:36. [Supplement.]

A lovely carriage.

1 O 'Tis a lovely thing to see
A man of prudent heart,
Whose thoughts, and lips, and life agree
To act a useful part.

2 When envy, strife, and wars begin,
In little angry souls,

Mark how the sons of peace come in,
And quench the kindling coals.

3 Their minds are humble, mild, and meek,
Nor let their fury rise;
Nor passion moves their lips to speak,
Nor pride exalts their eyes.

4 Their frame is prudence mix'd with love,
Good works fulfil their day:
They join the serpent with the dove,
But cast the sting away.

5 Such was the Saviour of mankind;
Such pleasures he pursu'd;
His flesh and blood were all refin'd,
His soul divinely good.

6 Lord, can these plants of virtue grow
In such a heart as mine?
Thy grace my nature can renew,
And make my soul like thine.

Hymn 1:37. [Supplement.]

Zeal and Fortitude.

1 Do I believe what Jesus saith,
And think the gospel true?
Lord, make me bold to own my faith,
And practise virtue too.

2 Suppress my shame, subdue my fear,
Arm me with heavenly zeal,
That I may make thy power appear,
And works of praise fulfil.

3 If men shall see my virtue shine,
And spread my name abroad,
Thine is the power, the praise is thine,
My Saviour and my God.

4 Thus when the saints in glory meet,
Their lips proclaim thy grace;
They cast their honours at thy feet,
And own their borrow'd rays.

PAUSE.

5 Are we the soldiers of the cross?
The followers of the Lamb?
And shall we fear to own his cause,
Or blush to speak his name?

6 Now we must fight, if we would reign;
Increase our courage, Lord!

We'll bear the toil, endure the pain,
Supported by thy word.

7 Thy saints in all this glorious war
Shall Conquer tho' they're slain;
They see the triumph from afar,
And shall with Jesus reign.

8 When that illustrious day shall rise,
And all thy armies shine
In robes of victory thro' the skies,
The glory shall be thine.

Hymn 1:38. [Supplement.]

The universal law of equity. Matt. 8. 12.

1 Blessed Redeemer how divine,
How righteous is this rule of thine,
"To do to all men just the same
"As we expect or wish from them."

2 This golden lesson, short and plain,
Gives not the mind nor memory
pain;
And every conscience must
approve
This universal law of love.

3 How blest would every nation be,
Thus rul'd by love and equity!
All would be friends without a foe,
And form a paradise below.

4 Jesus, forgive us, that we keep
Thy sacred law of love asleep,
No more let envy, wrath, and pride,
But thy blest maxims be our guide.

Hymn 1:39.

God's tender care of his church, Isa. 13 &c.

1 How shall my inward joys arise
And burst into a song,
Almighty love inspires my heart,
And pleasure tunes my tongue.

2 God on his thirsty Sion-hill
Some mercy-drops has thrown,
And solemn oaths have bound his love
To shower salvation down.

3 Why do we then indulge our fears,
Suspicions and complaints?
Is he a God, and shall his grace
Grow weary of his saints?

4 Can a kind woman e'er forget
The infant of her womb,
And 'mongst a thousand tender thoughts
Her suckling have no room?

5 "Yet (saith the Lord) should nature change,
"And mothers monsters prove,
"Sion still dwells upon the heart
"Of everlasting love.

6 "Deep on the palms of both my hands
"I have engrav'd her name,
"My hands shall raise her ruin'd walls,
"And build her broken frame."

Hymn 1:40.

The business and blessedness of glorified saints, Rev. 7. 13 &c.

1 "What happy men, or angels these
"That all their robes are spotless white?
"Whence did this glorious troop arrive
"At the pure realms of heavenly light?"

2 From tort'ring racks and burning fires,
And seas of their own blood they
came;
But nobler blood has wash'd their
robes,
Flowing from Christ the dying Lamb.

3 Now they approach th' almighty
throne,
With loud hosannas night and day,
Sweet anthems to the great Three
One
Measure their blest eternity.

4 No more shall hunger pain their
souls,
He bids their parching thirst be
gone,
And spreads the shadow of his
wings
To screen them from the scorching
sun.

5 The Lamb that fills the middle throne
Shall shed around his milder beams,
There shall they feast on his rich
love,
And drink full joys from living
streams.

6 Thus shall their mighty bliss renew
Thro' the vast round of endless years,
And the soft hand of sovereign grace
Heals all their wounds, and wipes their tears.

Hymn 1:41.

The same; or, The martyrs glorified, Rev. 7. 13 &c.

1 "These glorious minds, how bright they shine
"Whence all their white array?
"How came they to the happy seats
"Of everlasting day?"

2 From tort'ring pains to endless joys
On fiery wheels they rode,
And strangely wash'd their raiment white
In Jesus' dying blood.

3 Now they approach a spotless God,
And bow before his throne
Their warbling harps and sacred songs
Adore the Holy One.

4 The unveil'd glories of his face
Amongst his saints reside,
While the rich treasure of his grace
Sees all their wants supply'd.

5 Tormenting thirst shall leave their souls,
And hunger flee as fast;
The fruit of life's immortal tree
Shall be their sweet repast.

6 The Lamb shall lead his heavenly flock
Where living fountains rise,
And love divine shall wipe away
The sorrows of their eyes.

Hymn 1:42.

Divine wrath and mercy, Nahum 1, 2 &c.

1 Adore and tremble, for our God
Is a *consuming fire*;*
His jealous eyes his wrath inflame,
And raise his vengeance higher.

2 Almighty vengeance how it burns!
How bright his fury glows!

* Hebrews 12:29.

Vast magazines of plagues and
  storms
Lie treasur'd for his foes.

3 Those heaps of wrath by slow
  degrees
Are forced into a flame,
But kindled, O how fierce they blaze!
And rend all nature's frame.

4 At his approach the mountains flee,
And seek a watery grave;
The frighted sea makes haste away,
And shrinks up every wave.

5 Thro' the wide air the weighty rocks
Are swift as hailstones hurl'd:
Who dares engage his fiery rage
That shakes the solid world?

6 Yet, mighty God, thy sovereign grace
Sits regent on the throne,
The refuge of thy chosen race
When wrath comes rushing down.

7 Thy hand shall on rebellious kings
A fiery tempest pour,
While we beneath thy sheltering wings
Thy just revenge adore.

Hymn 1:43. [Supplement.]

The Christian treasure, 1 Cor. 3. 21.

1 How vast the treasure we possess!
How rich thy bounty, King of Grace!
This world is ours, and worlds
to come
Earth is our lodge, and heaven our
home.

2 All things are ours, the gifts of God;
The purchase of a Saviour's blood:
While the good Spirit shews us how
To use and to improve them too.

3 If peace and plenty crown my days,
They help, me, Lord, to speak thy
praise!
If bread of sorrows be my food,
Those sorrows work my lasting good.

4 I would not change my blest estate
For all the world calls good or great:
And while my faith can keep her hold,
I envy not the sinner's gold.

5 Father, I wait thy daily will;
Thou shalt divide my portion still:

Grant me on earth what seems
thee best,
Till death and heaven reveal the rest.

Hymn 1:44. [Supplement.]

The true improvement of life.

1 And is this life prolong'd to me?
Are days and seasons given?
O let me then prepare to be
A fitter heir of heaven.

2 In vain these moments shall
not pass,
These golden hours be gone:
Lord, I accept thine offered grace,
I bow before thy throne.

3 Now cleanse my soul from every sin,
By my Redeemer's blood:
Now let my flesh and soul begin
The honours of my God.

4 Let me no more my soul beguile
With sin's deceitful toys:
Let cheerful hope increasing still
Approach to heavenly joys.

5 My thankful lips shall loud proclaim
The wonders of thy praise,
And spread the savour of thy Name
Where'er I spend my days.

6 On earth let my example shine,
And when I leave this state,
May heaven receive this soul of mine
To bliss supremely great.

Hymn 1:45.

The last judgment, Rev. 21. 5-8.

1 See where the great incarnate God
Fills a majestic throne,
While from the skies his awful voice
Bears the last judgment down.

2 ["I am the first, and I the last,
"Thro' endless years the same;
"I AM is my memorial still,
"And my eternal name.

3 "Such favours as a God can give
"My royal grace bestows;
"Ye thirsty souls come taste the streams
"Where life and pleasure flows.]

4 ["The saint that triumphs o'er his sins,
"I'll own him for a son,
"The whole creation shall reward
"The conquests he has won.

5 "But bloody hands and hearts unclean,
"And all the lying race,
"The faithless and the scoffing crew,
"That spurn at offer'd grace,

6 "They shall be taken from my sight,
"Bound fast in iron chains,
"And headlong plung'd into the lake
"Where fire and darkness reigns."

7 O may I stand before the Lamb,
When earth and seas are fled!
And hear the Judge pronounce my name
With blessings on my head!

8 May I with those for ever dwell
Who here were my delight,
While sinners banish'd down to hell,
No more offend my sight.

Hymn 1:46. [Supplement.]

The privileges of the living above the dead.

1 Awake, my zeal, awake, my love,
To serve my Saviour here below,
In works which perfect saints above
And holy angels cannot do.

2 Awake my charity, to feed
The hungry soul, and clothe the poor:
In heaven are found no sons of need,
There all these duties are no more.

3 Subdue thy passions, O my soul!
Maintain the fight, thy work pursue,
Daily thy rising sins control,
And be thy victories ever new.

4 The land of triumph lies on high,
There are no foes t' encounter there:
Lord, I would conquer till I die,
And finish all the glorious war.

5 Let every flying hour confess
I gain thy gospel fresh renown;
And when my life and labour cease,
May I possess the promis'd crown.

Hymn 1:47. [Supplement.]

Death of kindred improved.

1 Must friends and kindred drop and die?
And helpers be withdrawn?
While sorrow with a weeping eye
Counts up our comforts gone?

2 Be thou our comfort, mighty God!
Our helper and our friend:
Nor leave us in this dangerous road,
Till all our trials end.

3 O may our feet pursue the way
Our pious fathers led!
With love and holy zeal obey
The counsels of the dead.

4 Let us be wean'd from all below,
Let hope our grief expel,
While death invites our souls to go
Where our best kindred dwell.

Hymn 1:48.

The Christian race, Isa. 40. 28-31.

1 Awake, our souls, away, our fears,
Let every trembling thought be gone;
Awake and run the heavenly race,
And put a cheerful courage on.

2 True, 'Tis a strait and thorny road,
And mortal spirits tire and faint;
But they forget the mighty God
That feeds the strength of every saint.

3 Thee, mighty God, whose matchless
power
Is ever new and ever young,
And firm endures while endless years
Their everlasting circles run.

4 From thee the overflowing spring,
Our souls shall drink a fresh supply,
While such as trust their native
strength
Shall melt away, and drop and die.

5 Swift as an eagle cuts the air
We'll mount aloft to thine abode,
On wings of love our souls shall fly,
Nor tire amidst the heavenly road.

Hymn 1:49.

The works of Moses and the Lamb, Rev. 15. 3.

1 How strong thine arm is, mighty God,
Who would not fear thy Name!

Jesus, how sweet thy graces are!
Who would not love the Lamb!

2 He has done more than Moses did,
Our Prophet and our King;
From bonds of hell he freed our souls,
And taught our lips to sing.

3 In the Red-sea by Moses' hand
Th' Egyptian host was drown'd;
But his own blood hides all our sins,
And guilt no more is found.

4 When thro' the desert Israel went,
With manna they were fed;
Our Lord invites us to his flesh,
And calls it living bread.

5 Moses beheld the promis'd land,
Yet never reach'd the place;
But Christ shall bring his followers home
To see his Father's face.

6 Then shall our love and joy be full,
And feel a warmer flame;
And sweeter voices tune the song
Of Moses and the Lamb.

Hymn 1:50.

The song of Zacharias, and the message of John the Baptist; or, Light and salvation by Jesus Christ, Luke 1. 68 &c. John 1. 29. 32.

1 Now be the God of Israel bless'd
Who makes his truth appear,
His mighty hand fulfils his word,
And all the oaths he sware.

2 Now he bedews old David's root
With blessings from the skies;
He makes the branch of promise grow,
The promis'd horn arise.

3 [John was the prophet of the Lord
To go before his face,
The herald which our Saviour God
Sent to prepare his ways.

4 He makes the great salvation known,
He speaks of pardon'd sins;
While grace divine and heavenly love
In its own glory shines.

5 "Behold the Lamb of God," he cries,
"That takes our guilt away:
"I saw the Spirit o'er his head
"On his baptizing day.]

6 "Be every vale exalted high,
"Sink every mountain low,
"The proud must stoop, and humble souls
"Shall his salvation know.

7 "The heathen realms with Israel's land
"Shall join in sweet accord;
"And all that's born of man shall see
"The glory of the Lord.

8 "Behold the morning star arise,
"Ye that in darkness sit;
"He marks the path that leads to peace,
"And guides our doubtful feet."

Hymn 1:51.

Persevering grace, Jude 24 25.

1 To God the only wise,
Our Saviour and our King,

Let all the saints below the skies
Their humble praises bring.

2 'Tis his almighty love,
His counsel, and his care,
Preserves us safe from sin and
  death,
And every hurtful snare.

3 He will present our souls
Unblemish'd and complete,
Before the glory of his face,
With joys divinely great.

4 Then all the chosen seed
Shall meet around the throne,
Shall bless the conduct of his
  grace,
And make his wonders known.

5 To our Redeemer God
Wisdom and power belongs,
Immortal crowns of majesty,
And everlasting songs.

Hymn 1:52.

Baptism, Matt. 28. 19. Acts 2. 38.

1 'Twas the commission of our Lord,
"Go, teach the nations, and baptize;"
The nations have receiv'd the word
Since he ascended to the skies.

2 He sits upon th' eternal hills,
With grace and pardon in his hands,
And sends his covenant with the seals,
To bless the distant British lands.

3 "Repent, and be baptiz'd, (he saith)
For the remission of your sins;"
And thus our sense assists our faith,
And shews us what his gospel means.

4 Our souls he washes in his blood,
As water makes the body clean;
And the good Spirit from our God
Descends like purifying rain.

5 Thus we engage ourselves to thee,
And seal our covenant with the Lord:
O may the great eternal Three
In heaven our solemn vows record!

Hymn 1:53.

The Holy Scriptures, Heb. 1. 1 2. 2 Tim. 3. 15 16. Psalm 147. 19 20.

1 God who in various methods told
His mind and will to saints of old,
Sent down his Son, with truth and
grace,
To teach us in these latter days.

2 Our nation reads the written word,
That book of life, that sure record:
The bright inheritance of heaven
Is by the sweet conveyance given.

3 God's kindest thoughts are here
express'd,
Able to make us wise and bless'd;
The doctrines are divinely true,
Fit for reproof, and comfort too.

4 Ye British isles, who read his love
In long epistles from above,
(He hath not sent his sacred word
To every land) Praise ye the Lord.

Hymn 1:54.

Electing grace; or, Saints beloved in
Christ, Eph. 1. 3 &c.

1 Jesus, we bless thy Father's Name;
Thy God and ours are both the same:

What heavenly blessings from his
  throne
Flow down to sinners thro' his Son!

2 "Christ be my first elect," he said,
Then chose our souls in Christ
  our head,
Before he gave the mountains birth,
Or laid foundations for the earth.

3 Thus did eternal love begin
To raise us up from death and sin;
Our characters were then decreed,
"Blameless in love, a holy seed."

4 Predestinated to be sons,
Born by degrees, but chose at once;
A new regenerated race
To praise the glory of his grace.

5 With Christ our Lord we share our part
In the affections of his heart,
Nor shall our souls be thence remov'd
Till he forgets his first belov'd.

Hymn 1:55.

Hesekiah's song; or, Sickness and recovery, Isa. 38.9 &c.

1 When we are rais'd from deep
distress
Our God deserves a song;
We take the pattern of our praise
From Hezekiah's tongue.

2 The gates of the devouring grave
Are open'd wide in vain,
If he that holds the keys of death
Commands them fast again.

3 Pains of the flesh are wont t' abuse
Our minds with slavish fears,
"Our days are past, and we shall lose
"The remnant of our years."

4 We chatter with a swallow's voice,
Or like a dove we mourn,
With bitterness instead of joys,
Afflicted and forlorn.

5 Jehovah speaks the healing word,
And no disease withstands;
Fevers and plagues obey the Lord,
And fly at his commands.

6 If half the strings of life should
break,
He can our frame restore;

He casts our sins behind his back,
And they are found no more.

Hymn 1:56.

The song of Moses and the Lamb; or, Babylon falling, Rev. 15. 3. and chap. 16. 19. and 17. 6.

1 We sing the glories of thy love,
We sound thy dreadful Name;
The Christian church unites the songs
Of Moses and the Lamb.

2 Great God, how wondrous are thy works
Of vengeance and of grace!
Thou King of saints, Almighty Lord,
How just and true thy ways!

3 Who dares refuse to fear thy Name,
Or worship at thy throne?
Thy judgments speak thine holiness
Thro' all the nations known.

4 Great Babylon, that rules the earth,
Drunk with the martyrs' blood,
Her crimes shall speedily awake
The fury of our God.

5 The cup of wrath is ready mix'd,
And she must drink the dregs;
Strong is the Lord her sovereign Judge,
And shall fulfil the plagues.

Hymn 1:57.

Original sin; or, The first and second Adam, Rom. 5. 12. Psalm 51. 5. Job 11. 4.

1 Backward with humble shame we look
On our original;
How is our nature dash'd and broke
In our first father's fall!

2 To all that's good averse and blind,
But prone to all that's ill
What dreadful darkness veils our
mind!
How obstinate our will!

3 [Conceiv'd in sin (O wretched state!)
Before we draw our breath,
The first young pulse begins to beat
Iniquity and death.

4 How strong in our degenerate blood
The old corruption reigns,

And, mingling with the crooked flood,
Wanders thro' all our veins!]

5 Wild and unwholesome as the root
Will all the branches be;
How can we hope for living fruit
From such a deadly tree?

6 What mortal power from things
unclean
Can pure productions bring?
Who can command a vital stream
From an infected spring?]

7 Yet, mighty God, thy wondrous love
Can make our nature clean,
While Christ and grace prevail above
The tempter, death, and sin.

8 The second Adam shall restore
The ruins of the first,
Hosanna to that sovereign power
That new creates our dust.

Hymn 1:58.

The devil vanquished; or, Michael's war with the dragon, Rev. 12. 7.

1 Let mortal tongues attempt to sing
The wars of heaven, when Michael
stood
Chief general of th' Eternal King,
And fought the battles of our God.

2 Against the dragon and his host
The armies of the Lord prevail:
In vain they rage, in vain they boast,
Their courage sinks, their weapons
fail.

3 Down to the earth was Satan
thrown,
Down to the earth his legions fell;
Then was the trump of triumph
blown,
And shook the dreadful deeps of
hell.

4 Now is the hour of darkness past,
Christ hath assum'd his reigning
power;
Behold the great accuser cast
Down from the skies, to rise no
more.

5 'Twas by thy blood immortal Lamb,
Thine armies trod the tempter down;

'Twas by thy word and powerful Name,
They gain'd the battle and renown.

6 Rejoice, ye heavens; let every star
Shine with new glories round the sky;
Saints, while ye sing the heavenly war,
Raise your Deliverer's name on high.

Hymn 1:59.

Babylon fallen, Rev. 18. 20 21.

1 In Gabriel's hand a mighty stone
Lies, a fair type of Babylon
''Prophets, rejoice, and, all ye saints,
"God shall avenge your long
complaints."

2 He said, and dreadful as he stood,
He sunk the milstone in the flood:
"Thus terribly shall Babel fall;
"Thus, and no more be found at all."

Hymn 1:60.

The virgin Mary's song; or, The
promised Messiah born, Luke 1. 46 &c.

1 Our souls shall magnify the Lord,
In God the Saviour we rejoice;
While we repeat the Virgin's song,
May the same spirit tune our voice.

2 [The Highest saw her low estate,
And mighty things his hand hath
done:
His overshadowing power and grace
Makes her the mother of his Son.

3 Let every nation call her bless'd,
And endless years prolong her fame;
But God alone must be ador'd;
Holy and reverend is his Name.]

4 To those that fear and trust the Lord
His mercy stands for ever sure:
From age to age his promise lives,
And the performance is secure.

5 He spake to Abr'am and his seed,
"In thee shall all the earth be
bless'd;"
The memory of that ancient word
Lay long in his eternal breast.

6 But now no more shall Israel wait,
No more the Gentiles lie forlorn:

Lo the desire of nations comes,
Behold the promis'd seed is born.

Hymn 1:61.

Christ our high Priest and King, and Christ coming to judgment, Rev. 1. 5 6 7.

1 Now to the Lord that makes us know
The wonders of his dying love,
Be humble honours paid below,
And strains of nobler praise above.

2 'Twas he that cleans'd our foulest sins,
And wash'd us in his richest blood;
'Tis he that makes us priests and kings,
And brings us rebels near to God.

3 To Jesus our atoning priest,
To Jesus our superior king,
Be everlasting power confess'd,
And every tongue his glory sing.

4 Behold, on flying clouds he comes,
And every eye shall see him move;
Tho' with our sins we pierc'd him once,
Then he displays his pardoning love.

5 The unbelieving world shall wail
While we rejoice to see the day:
Come, Lord; nor let thy promise fail,
Nor let thy chariots long delay.

Hymn 1:62.

Christ Jesus, the Lamb of God, worshipped by all the creation, Rev. 5. 11 12 13.

1 Come let us join our cheerful songs
With angels round the throne;
Ten thousand thousand are their
  tongues,
But all their joys are one.

2 "Worthy the Lamb that dy'd," they cry,
"To be exalted thus:"
"Worthy the Lamb," our lips reply,
"For he was slain for us."

3 Jesus is worthy to receive
Honour and power divine;
And blessings more than we can give,
Be, Lord, for ever thine.

4 Let all that dwell above the sky,
And air, and earth, and seas,

Conspire to lift thy glories high,
And speak thine endless praise.

5 The whole creation join in one
To bless the sacred Name
Of him that sits upon the throne,
And to adore the Lamb.

Hymn 1:63.

Christ's humiliation and exaltation,
Rev. 5. 12.

1 What equal honours shall we bring
To thee, O Lord our God, the Lamb,
When all the notes that angels sing
Are far inferior to thy Name?

2 Worthy is he that once was slain,
The Prince of Peace that groan'd
and dy'd,
Worthy to rise, and live, and reign
At his Almighty Father's side.

3 Power and dominion are his due,
Who stood condemn'd at Pilate's
bar:
Wisdom belongs to Jesus too,

Tho' he was charg'd with madness
here.

4 All riches are his native right,
Yet he sustain'd amazing loss:
To him ascribe eternal might,
Who left his weakness on the
cross.

5 Honour immortal must be paid,
Instead of scandal and of scorn:
While glory shines around his
head,
And a bright crown without a
thorn.

6 Blessings for ever on the Lamb,
Who bore the curse for wretched
men:
Let angels sound his sacred Name,
And every creature say, Amen.

Hymn 1:64.

Adoption, 1 John 3. 1 &c. Gal. 4. 6.

1 Behold what wondrous grace
The Father hath bestow'd

On sinners of a mortal race,
To call them sons of God!

2 'Tis no surprising thing
That we should be unknown;
The Jewish world knew not their
  King,
God's everlasting Son.

3 Nor doth it yet appear
How great we must be made;
But when we see our Saviour here,
We shall be like our head.

4 A hope so much divine
May trials well endure,
May purge our souls from sense
  and sin,
As Christ the Lord is pure.

5 If in my Father's love
I share a filial part,
Send down thy Spirit like a dove
To rest upon my heart.

6 We would no longer lie
Like slaves beneath the throne;
My faith shall Abba, Father, cry,
And thou the kindred own.

Hymn 1:65.

The kingdoms of the world become the kingdoms of our Lord; or, The day of judgment, Rev. 11. 15-18.

1 Let the seventh angel sound on high,
Let shouts be heard thro' all
the sky;
Kings of the earth, with glad
accord
Give up your kingdoms to the Lord.

2 Almighty God, thy power assume,
Who wast, and art, and art to come:
Jesus, the Lamb, who once was slain,
For ever live, for ever reign.

3 The angry nations fret and roar,
That they can slay the saints no
more;
On wings of vengeance flies
our God
To pay the long arrears of blood.

4 Now must the rising dead appear,
Now the decisive sentence hear;
Now the dear martyrs of the Lord
Receive an infinite reward.

Hymn 1:66.

Christ the King at his table, Cant. (Transcriber's Note: Song of Solomon) 1. 2-5 12 13 17.

1 Let him embrace my soul, and prove
Mine interest in his heavenly love:
The voice that tells me, "Thou art mine,"
Exceeds the blessings of the vine.

2 On thee th' anointing Spirit came,
And spreads the savour of thyname;
That oil of gladness and of grace
Draws virgin souls to meet thy face.

3 Jesus, allure me by thy charms,
My soul shall fly into thine arms,
Our wandering feet thy favours bring
To the fair chambers of the King.

4 [Wonder and pleasure tune our voice
To speak thy praises and our joys:
Our memory keeps this love of thine
Beyond the taste of richest wine.]

5 Tho' in ourselves deform'd we are,
And black as Kedar tent appear,
Yet when we put thy beauties on,
Fair as the courts of Solomon.

6 While at his table sits the King,
He loves to see us smile and sing;
Our graces are our best perfume,
And breathe like spikenard round
the room.]

7 As myrrh new bleeding from the tree,
Such is a dying Christ to me;
And while he makes my soul his
guest,
My bosom, Lord, shall be thy rest.

8 [No beams of cedar or of fir
Can with thy courts on earth
compare;
And here we wait until thy love
Raise us to nobler seats above.]

Hymn 1:67.

Seeking the pastures of Christ the
Shepherd, Cant. 1.7.

1 Thou whom my soul admires above
All earthly joy, and earthly love,
Tell me, dear shepherd, let me know,
Where doth thy sweetest pasture grow?

2 Where is the shadow of that rock
That from the son defends thy flock?
Fain would I feed among thy sheep,
Among them rest, among them sleep.

3 Why should thy bride appear like one
That turns aside to paths unknown?
My constant feet would never rove,
Would never seek another love.

4 [The footsteps of thy flock I see;
Thy sweetest pastures here they be;
A wondrous feast thy love prepares,
Bought with thy wounds, and groans, and tears.

5 His dearest flesh he makes my food,
And bids me drink his richest blood;
Here to these hills my soul will come,
To my beloved lead me home.]

Hymn 1:68.

The banquet of love, Cant. 2. 1 2 3 4 6 7.

1 Behold the Rose of Sharon here,
The Lily which the vallies bear;
Behold the Tree of Life, that gives
Refreshing fruit and healing leaves.

2 Amongst the thorns so lilies shine,
Amongst wild gourds the noble vine;
So in mine eyes my Saviour proves
Amidst a thousand meaner loves.

3 Beneath his cooling shade I sat
To shield me from the burning heat;
Of heavenly fruit he spreads a feast
To feed my eyes and please my taste.

4 [Kindly he brought me to the place
Where stands the banquet of his grace,
He saw me faint, and o'er my head
The banner of his love he spread.

5 With living bread and generous wine
He cheers this sinking heart of mine;
And opening his own heart to me,
He shews his thoughts how kind
they be.]

6 O never let my Lord depart,
Lie down and rest upon my heart;
I charge my sins not once to move
Nor stir, nor wake, nor grieve
  my Love.

Hymn 1:69.

Christ appearing to his church, and seeking her company, Cant. 2. 1-13.

1 The voice of my beloved sounds
Over the rocks and rising grounds,
O'er hills of guilt, and seas of
  grief,
He leaps, he flies to my relief.

2 Now thro' the veil of flesh I see
With eyes of love he looks at me;
Now in the gospel's clearest glass
He shews the beauties of his face.

3 Gently he draws my heart along
Both with his beauties and his
  tongue;
"Rise," saith my Lord, "make haste
  away;
"No mortal joys are worth thy stay.

4 "The Jewish wintery state is gone,
"The mists are fled, the spring
comes on,
"The sacred turtle-dove we hear
"Proclaim the new, the joyful year.

5 "Th' immortal vine of heavenly root
"Blossoms and buds, and gives her
fruit:"
Lo, we are come to taste the wine;
Our souls rejoice and bless the vine.

6 And when we hear our Jesus say,
"Rise up, my love, make haste away!"
Our hearts would fain out-fly the
wind,
And leave all earthly loves behind.

Hymn 1:70.

Christ inviting, and the church answering the invitation, Cant. 2. 14 16 17.

1 [Hark, the Redeemer from on high
Sweetly invites his favourites nigh;
From caves of darkness and of
doubt,
He gently speaks, and calls us out:

2 “My dove, who hidest in the rock,
“Thine heart almost with sorrow broke,
“Lift up thy face, forget thy fear,
“And let thy voice delight mine ear.

3 “Thy voice to me sounds ever sweet;
“My graces in thy countenance
meet;
“Tho’ the vain world thy face
despise,
“’Tis bright and comely in mine
eyes.”

4 Dear Lord, our thankful heart receives
The hope thine invitation gives:
‘To thee our joyful lips shall raise
The voice of prayer, and of praise.]

5 [I am my Love’s, and he is mine;
Our hearts, our hopes, our passions
join:
Nor let a motion, nor a word,
Nor thought arise to grieve my Lord.

6 My soul to pastures fair he leads,
Amongst the lilies where he feeds;
Amongst the saints (whose robes
are white,
Wash’d in his blood) is his delight.

7 Till the day break, and shadows flee,
Till the sweet dawning light I see,
Thine eyes to me-ward often turn,
Nor let my soul in darkness mourn.

8 Be like a hart on mountains green,
Leap o'er the hills of fear and sin;
Nor guilt, nor unbelief divide
My Love, my Saviour from my side.]

Hymn 1:71.

Christ found in the street, and brought to the church, Cant. 3. 1-5.

1 Often I seek my Lord by night,
Jesus, my love, my soul's delight;
With warm desire and restless thought
I seek him oft, but find him not.

2 Then I arise, and search the street
Till I my Lord, my Saviour meet;
I ask the watchmen of the night,
"Where did you see my soul's
delight?"

3 Sometimes I find him in the way,
Directed by a heavenly ray;

I leap for joy to see his face,
And hold him fast in mine embrace.

4 [I bring him to my mother's home,
Nor does my Lord refuse to come,
To Sion's sacred chambers, where
My soul first drew the vital air.

5 He gives me there his bleeding heart,
Pierc'd for my sake with deadly
smart;
I give my soul to him, and there
Our loves their mutual tokens
share.]

6 I charge you all, ye earthly toys,
Approach not to disturb my joys;
Nor sin, nor hell come near my
heart,
Nor cause my Saviour to depart.

Hymn 1:72.

The coronation of Christ, and espousals of the church, Cant. 3. 2.

1 Daughters of Sion, come, behold
The crown of honour and of gold,

Which the glad church with joys
  unknown
Plac'd on the head of Solomon.

2 Jesus, thou everlasting King,
Accept the tribute which we bring,
Accept the well-deserv'd renown,
And wear our praises as thy crown.

3 Let every act of worship be
Like our espousals, Lord, to thee;
Like the dear hour, when from above
We first receiv'd thy pledge of love.

4 The gladness of that happy day,
Our hearts would wish it long to
  stay,
Nor let our faith forsake its hold,
Nor comfort sink, nor love grow
  cold.

5 Each following minute as it flies,
Increase thy praise, improve our
  joys,
Till we are rais'd to sing thy Name
At the great supper of the Lamb.

6 O that the months would roll away,
And bring that coronation-day!

The King of Grace shall fill the throne
With all his Father's glories on.

Hymn 1:73.

The church's beauty in the eyes of Christ, Cant. 4. 1 10 11 7 9 8.

1 Kind is the speech of Christ our Lord,
Affection sounds in every word,
"Lo, thou art fair, my love, he cries,
"Not the young doves have sweeter eyes.

2 ["Sweet are thy lips, thy pleasing voice
"Salutes mine ear with secret joys,
"No spice so much delights the smell,
"Nor milk nor honey taste so well.]

3 "Thou art all fair, my bride, to me,
"I will behold no spot in thee."
What mighty wonders love performs,
And puts a comeliness on worms!

4 Defil'd and loathsome as we are,
He makes us white, and calls us fair;

Adorns us with that heavenly dress,
His graces and his righteousness.

5 "My sister, and my spouse," he cries,
"Bound to my heart by various ties,
"Thy powerful love my heart detains
"In strong delight and pleasing
chains."

6 He calls me from the leopard's den,
From this wild world of beasts and
men,
To Sion where his glories are;
Not Lebanon is half so fair.

7 Nor dens of prey, nor flowery
plains
Nor earthly joys, nor earthly pains
Shall hold my feet, or force my stay,
When Christ invites my soul away.

Hymn 1:74.

The church the garden of Christ, Cant. 4. 12 14 15, and 5. 1.

1 We are a garden wall'd around,
Chosen and made peculiar ground;

A little spot inclos'd by grace,
Out of the world's wide wilderness.

2 Like trees of myrrh and spice we
  stand,
Planted by God the Father's hand;
And all his springs in Sion flow
To make the young plantation grow.

3 Awake, O heavenly wind, and come,
Blow on this garden of perfume;
Spirit divine, descend and breathe
A gracious gale on plants beneath.

4 Make our best spices flow abroad
To entertain our Saviour God:
And faith, and love, and joy appear,
And every grace be active here.

5 [Let my beloved come, and taste
His pleasant fruits at his own feast:
"I come, my spouse, I come," he cries,
With love and pleasure in his eyes.

6 Our Lord into his garden comes,
Well pleas'd to smell our poor
  perfumes;
And calls us to a feast divine,
Sweeter than honey, milk, or wine.

7 "Eat of the tree of life, my friends,
"The blessings that my Father sends;
"Your taste shall all my dainties prove,
"And drink abundance of my love."

8 Jesus, we will frequent thy board,
And sing the bounties of our Lord:
But the rich food on which we live
Demands more praise than tongues can give.]

Hymn 1:75.

The description of Christ the beloved, Cant. 5. 9-12 14 15 16.

1 The wondering world enquires to know
Why I should love my Jesus so:
"What are his charms," say they, "above
"The objects of a mortal love!"

2 Yes, my beloved, to my sight,
Shews a sweet mixture red and white:

All human beauties, all divine,
In my beloved meet and shine,

3 White is his soul, from blemish free;
Red with the blood he shed for me;
The fairest of ten thousand fairs:
A sun amongst ten thousand stars.

4 [His head the finest gold excels,
There wisdom in perfection dwells;
And glory like a crown adorns
Those temples once beset with
thorns.

5 Compassions in his heart are found,
Hard by the signals of his wound;
His sacred side no more shall bear
The cruel scourge, the piercing
spear.]

6 [His hands are fairer to behold
Than diamonds set in rings of gold;
Those heavenly hands that on the
tree
Were nail'd, and torn, and bled for
me.

7 Tho' once he bow'd his feeble knees,
Loaded with sins and agonies,

Now on the throne of his command
His legs like marble pillars stand.]

8 [His eyes are majesty and love,
The eagle temper'd with the dove:
No more shall trickling sorrows roll
Thro' those dear windows of his soul.

9 His mouth, that pour'd out long
complaints,
Now smiles, and cheers his fainting
saints;
His countenance more graceful is
Than Lebanon with all its trees.]

10 All over glorious is my Lord,
Must be belov'd, and yet ador'd:
His worth if all the nations knew,
Sure the whole earth would love him
too.

Hymn 1:76.

Christ dwells in heaven, but visits on earth, Cant. 6. 1 2 3 12.

1 When strangers stand and hear me tell
What beauties in my Saviour dwell;

Where he is gone, they fain would
know,
That they may seek and love him too.

2 My best beloved keeps his throne
On hills of light in worlds unknown
But he descends, and shews his face
In the young gardens of his grace.

3 [In vineyards planted by his hand,
Where fruitful trees in order stand;
He feeds among the spicy beds,
Where lilies shew their spotless
heads.

4 He has engross'd my warmest love,
No earthly charms my soul can
move:
I have a mansion in his heart,
Nor death nor hell shall make us
part.]

5 [He takes my soul ere I'm aware,
And shews me where his glories are;
No chariot of Amminadib
The heavenly rapture can describe.

6 O may my spirit daily rise
On wings of faith above the skies,

Till death shall make my last remove
To dwell for ever with my love.]

Hymn 1:77.

The love of Christ to the church, in his language to her, and provisions for her, Cant. 7. 5 6 9 12 13.

1 Now in the galleries of his grace
Appears the King, and thus he says,
"How fair my saints are in my sight;
"My love how pleasant for delight!"

2 Kind is thy language, sovereign Lord,
There's heavenly grace in every word:
From that dear mouth a stream divine
Flows sweeter than the choicest
wine.

3 Such wondrous love awakes the lip
Of saints that were almost asleep,
To speak the praises of thy name,
And makes our cold affections
flame.

4 These are the joys he lets us know
In fields and villages below,

Gives us a relish of his love,
But keeps his noblest feast above.

5 In Paradise within the gates
An higher entertainment waits;
Fruits new and old laid up in store,
Where we shall feed, but thirst no more.

Hymn 1:78.

The strength of Christ's love, and the soul's jealousy of her own, Cant. 8. 5 6 7 13 14.

1 [Who is this fair one in distress,
That travels from the wilderness?
And press'd with sorrows and with sins,
On her beloved Lord she leans.

2 This is the spouse of Christ our God,
Bought with the treasure of his blood;
And her request and her complaint
Is but the voice of every saint.]

3 "O let my name engraven stand,
"Both on thy heart and on thy hand:

"Seal me upon thine arm; and wear
"That pledge of love for ever there.

4 "Stronger than death thy love is
known,
"Which floods of wrath could never
drown;
"And hell and earth in vain
combine
"To quench a fire so much divine.

5 "But I am jealous of my heart,
Lest it should once from thee
depart;
"Then let thy name be well
impress'd
As a fair signet on my breast.

6 "Till thou hast brought me to thy
home,
"Where fears and doubts can never
come,
"Thy count'nance let me often see,
"And often thou shalt hear from me.

7 "Come, my beloved, haste away,
"Cut short the hours of thy delay,
"Fly like a youthful hart or roe
"Over the hills where spices grow."

Hymn 1:79.

A morning hymn, Psalm 19. 5 8 and 73. 24 25.

1 God of the morning, at whose voice
The cheerful sun makes haste to rise,
And, like a giant doth rejoice
To run his journey thro' the skies;

2 From the fair chambers of the east
The circuit of his race begins,
And without weariness or rest,
Round the whole earth he flies and shines.

3 O like the sun may I fulfil
Th' appointed duties of the day,
With ready mind and active will
March on and keep my heavenly way.

4 [But I shall rove and lose the race,
If God my sun should disappear,
And leave me in this world's wild maze,
To follow every wandering star.

5 Lord, thy commands are clean and pure,
Enlightening our beclouded eyes,

Thy threatenings just, thy promise
 sure,
Thy gospel makes the simple wise.]

6 Give me thy counsels for my guide,
And then receive me to thy bliss;
All my desires and hopes beside
Are faint and cold compar'd to this.

Hymn 1:80.

An evening hymn, Psalm 4. 8. and 3. 5
6. and 143. 8.

1 Thus far the Lord has led me on,
Thus far his power prolongs my days,
And every evening shall make known
Some fresh memorial of his grace.

2 Much of my time has run to waste,
And I perhaps am near my home;
But he forgives my follies past,
He gives me strength for days to come.

3 I lay my body down to sleep,
Peace is the pillow for my head,
While well-appointed angels keep
Their watchful stations round my bed.

4 In vain the sons of earth or hell
Tell me a thousand frightful things,
My God in safety makes me dwell
Beneath the shadow of his wings.

5 [Faith in his name forbids my fear:
O may thy presence ne'er depart!
And in the morning make me hear
The love and kindness of thy heart.

6 Thus when the night of death shall
come,
My flesh shall rest beneath the ground,
And wait thy voice to rouse my tomb,
With sweet salvation in the sound.

Hymn 1:81.

A song for morning or evening, Lam. 3. 23. Isa. 45. 7.

1 My God, how endless is thy love!
Thy gifts are every evening new;
And morning mercies from above
Gently distil like early dew.

2 Thou spreadst the curtains of the night,
Great guardian of my sleeping hours;

Thy sovereign word restores the light,
And quickens all my drowsy powers.

3 I yield my powers to thy command,
To thee I consecrate my days;
Perpetual blessings from thine hand
Demand perpetual songs of praise.

Hymn 1:82.

God far above creatures; or, Man vain and mortal, Job 4. 77-21.

1 Shall the vile race of flesh and blood
Contend with their creator, God?
Shall mortal worms presume to be
More holy, wise, or just than he?

2 Behold he puts his trust in none
Of all the spirits round his throne;
Their natures, when compar'd with his
Are neither holy, just nor wise.

3 But how much meaner things are they
Who spring from dust and dwell in clay!

Touch'd by the finger of thy wrath,
We faint and vanish like the moth.

4 From night to day, from day to night,
We die by thousands in thy sight;
Bury'd in dust whole nations lie
Like a forgotten vanity.

5 Almighty power, to thee we bow;
How frail are we, how glorious thou!
No more the sons of earth shall dare
With an eternal God compare.

Hymn 1:83.

Afflictions and death under providence, Job 5. 6 7 8.

1 Not from the dust affliction grows,
Nor troubles rise by chance;
Yet we are born to care and woes,
A sad inheritance.

2 As sparks break out from burning coals,
And still are upwards borne;
So grief is rooted in our souls,
And man grows up to mourn.

3 Yet with my God I leave my cause,
And trust his promis'd grace;
He rules me by his well-known laws
Of love and righteousness.

4 Not all the pains that e'er I bore
Shall spoil my future peace,
For death and hell can do no more
Than what my Father please.

Hymn 1:84.

Salvation, righteousness, and strength in Christ, Isa. 45. 21 25.

1 Jehovah speaks, let Israel hear,
Let all the earth rejoice and fear,
While God's eternal Son proclaims
His sovereign honours and his names:

2 "I am the last, and I the first,
"The Saviour God, and God the just;
"There's none beside pretends to shew
"Such justice and salvation too.

3 "[Ye that in shades of darkness dwell,
"Just on the verge of death and hell,

"Look up to me from distant lands,
"Light, life and heaven are in my
hands.

4 "I by my holy Name have sworn,
"Nor shall the word in vain return,
"To me shall all things bend the knee,
"And every tongue shall swear to
me.]

5 "In me alone shall men confess
"Lies all their strength and
righteousness;
"But such as dare despise my Name,
"I'll clothe them with eternal shame.

6 "In me the Lord, shall all the seed
"Of Israel from their sins be freed,
"And by their shining graces prove
"Their interest in my pardoning
love."

Hymn 1:85.

The same.

1 The Lord on high proclaims
His Godhead from his throne;

"Mercy and justice are the names
"By which I will be known.

2 "Ye dying souls that sit
"In darkness and distress,
"Look from the borders of the pit
"To my recovering grace."

3 Sinners shall hear the sound;
Their thankful tongues shall own,
"Our righteousness and strength is found
"In thee, the Lord, alone."

4 In thee shall Israel trust,
And see their guilt forgiven;
God will pronounce the sinners just,
And take the saints to heaven.

Hymn 1:86.

God holy, just, and sovereign. Job 9. 2-10.

1 How should the sons of Adam's race
Be pure before their God?
If he contend in righteousness
We fall beneath his rod.

2 To vindicate my words and
thoughts
I'll make no more pretence;
Not one of all my thousand faults
Can bear a just defence.

3 Strong is his arm, his heart is
wise;
What vain presumers dare
Against their Maker's hand to rise,
Or tempt th' unequal war?

4 [Mountains by his almighty wrath
From their old seats are torn;
He shakes the earth from south to
north,
And all her pillars mourn.

5 He bids the sun forbear to rise,
Th' obedient sun forbears:
His hand with sackcloth spreads the
skies,
And seals up all the stars.

6 He walks upon the stormy sea
Flies on the stormy wind;
There's none can trace his wondrous
way,
Or his dark footsteps find.]

Hymn 1:87.

God dwells with the humble and penitent, Isa. 57. 15 16.

1 Thus saith the High and Lofty One,
"I sit upon my holy throne,
"My name is God, I dwell on high,
"Dwell in my own eternity.

2 "But I descend to worlds below,
"On earth I have a mansion too,
"The humble spirit and contrite
"Is an abode of my delight.

3 "The humble soul my words revive,
"I bid the mourning sinner live,
"Heal all the broken hearts I find,
"And ease the sorrows of the mind.

4 "When I contend against their sin
"I make them know how vile they've been;
"But should my wrath for ever smoke,
"Their souls would sink beneath my stroke."]

5 O may thy pardoning grace be nigh,
Lest we should faint, despair, and
die!
Thus shall our better thoughts
approve
The methods of thy chastening love.

Hymn 1:88.

Life the day of grace and hope.
Eccles. 9. 4 3 6 10.

1 Life is the time to serve the Lord,
The time t' insure the great reward;
And while the lamp holds out to burn
The vilest sinner may return.

2 [Life is the hour that God has given
To 'scape from hell, and fly to
heaven,
The day of grace, and mortals may
Secure the blessings of the day.]

3 The living know that they must die,
But all the dead forgotten lie,
Their memory and their sense is
gone,
Alike unknowing and unknown.

4 [Their hatred and their love is lost,
Their envy bury'd in the dust;
They have no share in all that's done
Beneath the circuit of the sun.]

5 Then what my thoughts design to do,
My hands, with all your might pursue,
Since no device, nor work is found,
Nor faith, nor hope beneath the
ground.

6 There are no acts of pardon past
In the cold grave to which we haste,
But darkness, death, and long despair
Reign in eternal silence there.

Hymn 1:89.

Youth and judgment, Eccles. 11. 9.

1 Ye sons of Adam, vain and young,
Indulge your eyes, indulge your tongue,
Taste the delight your souls desire,
And give a loose to all your fire.

2 Pursue the pleasures ye design,
And cheer your hearts with songs
and wine,

Enjoy the day of mirth; but know
There is a day of judgment too.

3 God from on high beholds your thoughts,
His book records your secret faults;
The works of darkness you have done
Must all appear before the sun.

4 The vengeance to your follies due
Should strike your hearts with terror thro':
How will ye stand before his face,
Or answer for his injur'd grace?

5 Almighty God, turn off their eyes
From these alluring vanities;
And let the thunder of thy word
Awake their souls to fear the Lord.

Hymn 1:90.

The same.

1 Lo the young tribes of Adam rise,
And thro' all nature rove,
Fulfil the wishes of their eyes,
And taste the joys they love.

2 They give a loose to wild desires,
But let the sinners know,
The strict account that God requires
Of all the works they do.

3 The Judge prepares his throne on high,
The frighted earth and seas
Avoid the fury of his eye,
And flee before his face.

4 How shall I bear that dreadful day,
And stand the fiery test?
I give all mortal joys away
To be for ever blest.

Hymn 1:91.

Advice to youth; or, Old age and death in an unconverted state, Eccles. 12. 1 7. Isa. 65. 20.

1 Now in the heat of youthful blood
Remember your Creator God,
Behold the months come hastening on
When you shall say, "My joys are gone."

2 Behold, the aged sinner goes,
Laden with guilt and heavy woes

Down to the regions of the dead,
With endless curses on his head.

3 The dust returns to dust again,
The soul in agonies of pain
Ascends to God, not there to dwell,
But hears her doom, and sinks to
hell.

4 Eternal King! I fear thy Name,
Teach me to know how frail I am;
And when my soul must hence
remove,
Give me a mansion in thy love.

Hymn 1:92.

Christ the wisdom of God, Prov. 8. 1 22-32.

1 Shall wisdom cry aloud
And not her speech be heard?
The voice of God's eternal word,
Deserves it no regard?

2 "I was his chief delight,
"His everlasting Son,
"Before the first of all his works,
"Creation, was begun.

3 [“Before the flying clouds,
“Before the solid land,
“Before the fields, before the floods,
“I dwelt at his right hand.

4 “When he adorn’d the skies,
“And built them I was there
“To order where the sun should rise,
“And marshal every star.

5 “When he pour’d out the sea,
“And spread the flowing deep,
“I gave the flood a firm decree,
“In its own bounds to keep.]

6 “Upon the empty air
The earth was balanc’d well;
“With joy I saw the mansion where
“The sons of men should dwell.

7 “My busy thoughts at first
“On their salvation ran,
“Ere sin was born, or Adam’s dust
“Was fashioned to a man.

8 “Then come, receive my grace,
“Ye children, and be wise;
“Happy the man that keeps my ways;
“The man that shuns them dies.”

Hymn 1:93.

Christ, or wisdom, obeyed or resisted, Prov. 8. 31 35 36.

1 Thus saith the wisdom of the Lord,
"Bless'd is the man that hears my word,
"Keeps daily watch before my gates,
"And at my feet for mercy waits.

2 "The soul that seeks me shall obtain
"Immortal wealth and heavenly gain;
"Immortal life is his reward,
"Life, and the favour of the Lord.

3 "But the vile wretch that flies from me
"Doth his own soul an injury;
Fools that against my grace rebel
"Seek death, and love the road to hell."

Hymn 1:94.

Justification by faith, not by works; or, The law condemns, grace justifies, Rom. 3. 19-22.

1 Vain are the hopes the sons of men
On their own works have built;
Their hearts by nature all unclean,
And all their actions guilt.

2 Let Jew and Gentile stop their mouths
Without a murmuring word,
And the whole race of Adam stand
Guilty before the Lord.

3 In vain we ask God's righteous law
To justify us now,
Since to convince and to condemn
Is all the law can do.

4 Jesus, how glorious is thy grace,
When in thy name we trust,
Our faith receives a righteousness
That makes the sinner just.

Hymn 1:95.

Regeneration, John 1. 13. and 3. 3 &c.

1 Not all the outward forms on earth,
Nor rites that God has given,
Nor will of man, nor blood, nor birth,
Can raise a soul to heaven.

2 The sovereign will of God alone
Creates us heirs of grace;
Born in the image of his Son,
A new peculiar race.

3 The Spirit like some heavenly wind
Blows on the sons of flesh,
New models all the carnal mind,
And forms the man afresh.

4 Our quicken'd souls awake, and rise
From the long sleep of death;
On heavenly things we fix our eyes,
And praise employs our breath.

Hymn 1:96.

Election excludes boasting, 1 Cor. 1. 26-31.

1 But few among the carnal wise,
But few of noble race,
Obtain the favour of thine eyes,
Almighty King of Grace.

2 He takes the men of meanest name
For sons and heirs of God;
And thus he pours abundant shame
On honourable blood.

3 He calls the fool, and makes him know
The mysteries of his grace,
To bring aspiring wisdom low,
And all its pride abase.

4 Nature has all its glories lost
When brought before his throne;
No flesh shall in his presence boast
But in the Lord alone.

Hymn 1:97.

Christ our wisdom, righteousness,
&c. 1 Cor. 1. 30.

1 Bury'd in shadows of the night
We lie till Christ restores the light:
Wisdom descends to heal the blind,
And chase the darkness of the mind.

2 Our guilty souls are drown'd in tears
Till his atoning blood appears,
Then we awake from deep distress,
And sing, "The Lord our
Righteousness."

3 Our very frame is mix'd with sin,
His Spirit makes our natures clean;

Such virtues from his sufferings flow,
At once to cleanse and pardon too.

4 Jesus beholds where Satan reigns,
Binding his slaves in heavy chains;
He sets the prisoners free, and breaks
The iron bondage from our necks.

5 Poor helpless worms in thee possess
Grace, wisdom, power, and
righteousness;
Thou art our mighty All, and we
Give our whole selves, O Lord, to
thee.

Hymn 1:98.

The same.

1 How heavy is the night
That hangs upon our eyes,
Till Christ with his reviving light,
Over our souls arise!

2 Our guilty spirits dread
To meet the wrath of heaven
But, in his righteousness array'd,
We see our sins forgiven.

3 Unholy and impure
Are all our thoughts and ways;
His hands infected nature cure
With sanctifying grace.

4 The powers of hell agree
To hold our souls in vain;
He sets the sons of bondage free,
And breaks the cursed chain.

5 Lord, we adore thy ways
To bring us near to God,
Thy sovereign power, thy healing grace,
And thine atoning blood.

Hymn 1:99.

Stones made children of Abraham;
or, Grace not conveyed by religious
parents, Matt. 3. 9.

1 Vain are the hopes that rebels place
Upon their birth and blood,
Descended from a pious race;
(Their fathers now with God.)

2 He from the caves of earth and hell
Can take the hardest stones,

And fill the house of Abra'm well
With new-created sons.

3 Such wondrous power doth he possess
Who form'd our mortal frame,
Who call'd the world from emptiness,
The world obey'd and came.

Hymn 1:100.

Believe and be saved, John 3. 16 17 18.

1 Not to condemn the sons of men
Did Christ, the Son of God, appear;
No weapons in his hands are seen,
No flaming sword, nor thunder there.

2 Such was the pity of our God,
He lov'd the race of man so well,
He sent his Son to bear our load
Of sins, and save our souls from hell.

3 Sinners, believe the Saviour's word,
Trust in his mighty name and live;

A thousand joys his lips afford,
His hands a thousand blessings give.

4 But vengeance and damnation lies
On rebels who refuse the grace;
Who God's eternal Son despise
The hottest hell shall be their
place.

Hymn 1:101.

Joy in heaven for a repenting sinner,
Luke 15. 7-10.

1 Who can describe the joys that rise
Thro' all the courts of Paradise
To see a prodigal return,
To see an heir of glory born?

2 With joy the Father doth approve
The fruit of his eternal love;
The Son with joy looks down and sees
The purchase of his agonies.

3 The Spirit takes delight to view
The holy soul he form'd anew;
And saints and angels join to sing
The growing empire of their King.

Hymn 1:102.

The beatitudes, Matt. 5. 3-12.

1 [Bless'd are the humble souls that see
Their emptiness and poverty;
Treasures of grace to them are given,
And crowns of joy laid up in heaven.]

2 [Bless'd are the men of broken heart,
Who mourn for sin with inward smart;
The blood of Christ divinely flows,
A healing balm for all their woes.]

3 [Bless'd are the meek, who stand afar
From rage and passion, noise and war;
God will secure their happy state,
And plead their cause against the great.]

4 [Bless'd are the souls that thirst for grace,
Hunger and long for righteousness,
They shall be well supply'd and fed,
With living streams and living bread.]

5 [Bless'd are the men whose bowels
move
And melt with sympathy and love;
From Christ the Lord shall they obtain
Like sympathy and love again.]

6 [Bless'd are the pure, whose hearts
are clean
From the defiling powers of sin,
With endless pleasure they shall see
A God of spotless purity.]

7 [Bless'd are the men of peaceful life
Who quench the coals of growing strife,
They shall be call'd the heirs of bliss,
The sons of God, the God of peace.]

8 [Bless'd are the sufferers who partake
Of pain and shame for Jesus' sake;
Their souls shall triumph in the Lord,
Glory and joy are their reward.]

Hymn 1:103.

Not ashamed of the gospel, C Tim. 1. 12.

1 I'm not asham'd to own my Lord,
Or to defend his cause,

Maintain the honour of his word,
The glory of his cross.

2 Jesus, my God, I know his Name,
His Name is all my trust,
Nor will he put my soul to shame,
Nor let my hope be lost.

3 Firm as his throne his promise
stands,
And he can well secure
What I've committed to his hands
Till the decisive hour.

4 Then will he own my worthless name
Before his Father's face,
And in the new Jerusalem
Appoint my soul a place.

Hymn 1:104.

A state of nature and of grace, 1 Cor. 6. 10 11.

1 Not the malicious or profane,
The wanton or the proud,
Nor thieves, nor slanderers shall
obtain
The kingdom of our God.

2 Surprising grace! and such were we
By nature and by sin,
Heirs of immortal misery,
Unholy and unclean.

3 But we are wash'd in Jesus' blood,
We're pardon'd thro' his Name;
And the good Spirit of our God
Has sanctify'd our frame.

4 O for a persevering power
To keep thy just commands!
We would defile our hearts no
more,
No more pollute our hands.

Hymn 1:105.

Heaven invisible and holy, 1 Cor. 2. 9 10. Rev. 21. 27.

1 Nor eye has seen, nor ear has heard,
Nor sense nor reason known
What joys the Father hath prepar'd
For those that love the Son.

2 But the good Spirit of the Lord
Reveals a heaven to come:

The beams of glory in his word
Allure and guide us home.

3 Pure are the joys above the sky,
And all the region peace;
No wanton lips, nor envious eye
Can see or taste the bliss.

4 Those holy gates for ever bar
Pollution, sin, and shame;
None shall obtain admittance there
But followers of the Lamb.

5 He keeps the Father's book of life,
There all their names are found;
The hypocrite in vain shall strive
To tread the heavenly ground.

Hymn 1:106.

Dead to sin by the cross of Christ,
Rom. 6. 1 2 6.

1 Shall we go on to sin
Because thy grace abounds,
Or crucify the Lord again,
And open all his wounds?

2 Forbid it, mighty God,
Nor let it e'er be said
That we whose sins are crucify'd
Should raise them from the dead.

3 We will be slaves no more,
Since Christ has made us free,
Has nail'd our tyrants to his cross,
And bought our liberty.

Hymn 1:107.

The fall and recovery of man; or, Christ and Satan at enmity, Gen. 3 1 15 17 Gal. 4. 4. Col. 2. 15.

1 Deceiv'd by subtle snares of hell
Adam our head, our father fell,
When Satan in the serpent hid
Propos'd the fruit that God forbid.

2 Death was the threatening; death began
To take possession of the man;
His unborn race receiv'd the wound,
And heavy curses smote the ground.

3 But Satan found a worse reward;
Thus saith the vengeance of the Lord,
"Let everlasting hatred be
"Betwixt the woman's seed and thee.

4 "The woman's seed shall be my Son,
He shall destroy what thou hast
done,
"Shall break thy head, and only feel
"Thy malice raging at his heel."

5 [He spake; and bid four thousand years
Roll on;—at length his Son appears;
Angels with joy descend to earth,
And sing the young Redeemer's birth.

6 Lo, by the sons of hell he dies;
But, as he hung 'twixt earth and skies,
He gave their prince a fatal blow,
And triumph'd o'er the powers
below.]

Hymn 1:108.

Christ unseen and beloved, 1 Pet. 1. 8.

1 Not with our mortal eyes
Have we beheld the Lord,

Yet we rejoice to hear his Name,
And love him in his word.

2 On earth we want the sight
Of our Redeemer's face,
Yet, Lord, our inmost thoughts
 delight
To dwell upon thy grace.

3 And when we taste thy love,
Our joys divinely grow
Unspeakable, like those above,
And heaven begins below.

Hymn 1:109.

The value of Christ and his righteousness, Phil. 3. 7 8 9.

1 No more, my God, I boast no more
Of all the duties I have done;
I quit the hopes I held before
To trust the merits of thy Son.

2 Now for the love I bear his Name,
What was my gain I count my loss,
My former pride I call my shame,
And nail my glory to his cross.

3 Yes, and I must and will esteem
All things but loss for Jesus' sake
O may my soul be found in him,
And of his righteousness partake.

4 The best obedience of my hands
Dares not appear before thy throne;
But faith can answer thy demands
By pleading what my Lord has done.

Hymn 1:110.

Death and immediate glory, 2 Cor. 5. 1 5-8.

1 There is a house not made with hands,
Eternal and on high:
And here my spirit waiting stands
Till God shall bid it fly.

2 Shortly this prison of my clay
Must be dissolv'd and fall,
Then, O my soul, with joy obey
Thy heavenly Father's call.

3 'Tis he by his almighty grace
That forms thee fit for heaven,
And as an earnest of the place,
Has his own Spirit given.

4 We walk by faith of joys to come,
Faith lives upon his word;
But while the body is our home
We're absent from the Lord.

5 'Tis pleasant to believe thy grace,
But we had rather see;
We would be absent from the flesh,
And present, Lord, with thee.

Hymn 1:111.

Salvation by grace, Titus 3. 3-7.

1 [Lord, we confess our numerous faults,
How great our guilt has been!
Foolish and vain were all our
thoughts,
And all our lives were sin.

2 But O, my soul, for ever praise,
For ever love his Name,
Who turns thy feet from dangerous
ways
Of folly, sin, and shame.]

3 ['Tis not by works of righteousness
Which our own hands have done;

But we are sav'd by sovereign grace
Abounding thro' his Son.]

4 'Tis from the mercy of our God
That all our hopes begin;
'Tis by the water and the blood
Our souls are wash'd from sin.

5 'Tis thro' the purchase of his death,
Who hung upon the tree,
The Spirit is sent down to breathe
On such dry bones as we.

6 Rais'd from the dead we live anew;
And justify'd by grace
We shall appear in glory too,
And see our Father's face.

Hymn 1:112.

The brazen serpent; or, Looking to Jesus, John 3. 14 15 16.

1 So did the Hebrew prophet raise
The brazen serpent high,
The wounded felt immediate ease,
The camp forbore to die.

2 "Look upward in the dying hour,
And live," the prophet cries;
But Christ performs a nobler cure,
When Faith lifts up her eyes.

3 High on the cross the Saviour hung,
High in the heavens he reigns:
Here sinners by th' old serpent
stung
Look, and forget their pains.

4 When God's own Son is lifted up,
A dying world revives,
The Jew beholds the glorious hope,
Th' expiring Gentile lives.

Hymn 1:113.

Abraham's blessings on the Gentiles,
Gen. 17. 7. Rom. 15. 8. Mark 10. 14.

1 How large the promise! how divine,
To Abra'am and his seed!
"I'll be a God to thee and thine,
"Supplying all their need."

2 The words of his extensive love
From age to age endure;

The angel of the covenant proves,
And seals the blessing sure.

3 Jesus the ancient faith confirms
To our great fathers given;
He takes young children to his
arms,
And calls them heirs of heaven.

4 Our God, how faithful are his ways!
His love endures the same;
Nor from the promise of his grace
Blots out the children's name.

Hymn 1:114.

The same, Rom. 11. 16 17.

1 Gentiles by nature we belong
To the wild olive wood;
Grace took us from the barren tree,
And grafts us in the good.

2 With the same blessings grace
endows
The Gentile and the Jew;
If pure and holy be the root,
Such are the branches too.

3 Then let the children of the saints
Be dedicate to God;
Pour out thy Spirit on them, Lord,
And wash them in thy blood.

4 Thus to the parents and their seed
Shall thy salvation come,
And numerous households meet at last
In one eternal home.

Hymn 1:115.

Conviction of sin by the law,
Rom. 7. 8 9 14 24.

1 Lord, how secure my conscience was,
And felt no inward dread!
I was alive without the law,
And thought my sins were dead.

2 My hopes of heaven were firm and
bright,
But since the precept came
With a convincing power and light,
I find how vile I am.

3 [My guilt appear'd but small before,
Till terribly I saw

How perfect, holy, just, and pure,
Was thine eternal law.

4 Then felt my soul the heavy load,
My sins reviv'd again,
I had provok'd a dreadful God,
And all my hopes were slain.]

5 I'm like a helpless captive sold
Under the power of sin;
I cannot do the good I would,
Nor keep my conscience clean.

6 My God, I cry with every breath
For some kind power to save,
To break the yoke of sin and death,
And thus redeem the slave.

Hymn 1:116.

Love to God and our neighbour,
Matt. 22. 37-40.

1 Thus saith the first, the great
command,
"Let all thy inward powers unite
"To love thy Maker and thy God,
"With utmost vigour and delight.

2 "Then shall thy neighbour next in
place
"Share thine affections and esteem,
"And let thy kindness to thyself
"Measure and rule thy love to him."

3 This is the sense that Moses spoke,
This did the prophets preach and
prove,
For want of this the law is broke,
And the whole law's fulfill'd by love.

4 But O! how base our passions are!
How cold our charity and zeal!
Lord, fill our souls with heavenly
fire,
Or we shall ne'er perform thy will.

Hymn 1:117.

Election sovereign and free,
Rom. 9. 21 22 23 20.

1 Behold the potter and the clay,
He forms his vessels as he please:
Such is our God, and such are we,
The subjects of his high decrees.

2 [Doth not the workman's power extend
O'er all the mass, which part to choose,
And mould it for a nobler end,
And which to leave for viler use?]

3 May not the sovereign Lord on high
Dispense his favours as he will,
Choose some to life while others die,
And yet be just and gracious still?

4 [What if to make his terror known
He lets his patience long endure,
Suffering vile rebels to go on
And seal their own destruction sure!

5 What if he means to shew his grace,
And his electing love employs
To mark out some of mortal race,
And form them fit for heavenly joys!]

6 Shall man reply against the Lord,
And call his Maker's ways unjust,
The thunder of whose dreadful word
Can crush a thousand worlds to dust?

7 But, O my soul, if truths so bright
Should dazzle and confound thy sight
Yet still his written will obey,
And wait the great decisive day.

8 Then shall he make his justice known,
And the whole world before his
throne
With joy or terror shall confess
The glory of his righteousness.

Hymn 1:118.

Moses and Christ; or, Sins against the law and gospel, John 1. 17. Heb. 3. 3 5 6 and 10. 28 29.

1 The law by Moses came,
But peace, and truth, and love,
Were brought by Christ, a nobler
name,
Descending from above.

2 Amidst the house of God
Their different works were done;
Moses a faithful servant stood,
But Christ a faithful Son.

3 Then to his new commands
Be strict obedience paid;
O'er all his Father's house he
stands
The sovereign and the head.

4 The man that durst despise
The law that Moses brought,
Behold! how terribly he dies
For his presumptuous fault.

5 But sorer vengeance falls
On that rebellious race,
Who hate to hear when Jesus calls,
And dare resist his grace.

Hymn 1:119.

‘The different success of the gospel,
1 Cor. 1. 23 24. 2 Cor. 2. 16. 1 Cor. 3. 6 7.

1 Christ and his cross is all our
theme;
The mysteries that we speak
Are scandal in the Jew’s esteem,
And folly to the Greek.

2 But souls enlighten’d from above
With joy receive the word;
They see what wisdom, power, and love
Shines in their dying Lord.

3 The vital savour of his Name
Restores their fainting breath;

But unbelief perverts the same
To guilt, despair, and death.

4 Till God diffuse his graces down,
Like showers of heavenly rain,
In vain Apollos sows the ground,
And Paul may plant in vain.

Hymn 1:120.

Faith of things unseen, Heb. 11. 1 3 8 10.

1 Faith is the brightest evidence
Of things beyond our sight,
Breaks thro' the clouds of flesh and
sense,
And dwells in heavenly light.

2 It sets times past in present view,
Brings distant prospects home,
Of things a thousand years ago,
Or thousand years to come.

3 By faith we know the worlds were
made
By God's almighty word;
Abra'm to unknown countries led,
By faith obey'd the Lord.

4 He sought a city fair and high,
Built by th' eternal hands;
And faith assures us, tho' we die,
That heavenly building stands.

Hymn 1:121.

Children devoted to God, Gen. 17. 7 10. Acts 16. 14 15 33. (For those who practise infant Baptism.)

1 Thus saith the mercy of the Lord,
"I'll be a God to thee;
"I'll bless thy numerous race, and they
"Shall be a seed for me."

2 Abra'm believ'd the promis'd grace,
And gave his sons to God;
But water seals the blessing now,
That once was seal'd with blood.

3 Thus Lydia sanctify'd her house
When she receiv'd the word;
Thus the believing jailor gave
His household to the Lord.

4 Thus later saints, eternal King,
Thine ancient truth embrace;

To thee their infant-offspring bring,
And humbly claim the grace.

Hymn 1:122.

Believers buried with Christ in baptism, Rom. 6. 3 &c.

1 Do we not know that solemn word,
That we are bury'd with the Lord,
Baptis'd into his death, and then
Put off the body of our sin?

2 Our souls receive diviner breath,
Rais'd from corruption, guilt, and death;
So from the grave did Christ arise,
And lives to God above the skies.

3 No more let sin or Satan reign
Over our mortal flesh again;
The various lusts we serv'd before
Shall have dominion now no more.

Hymn 1:123.

The repenting prodigal, Luke 15. 13 &c.

1 Behold the wretch whose lust and wine
Had wasted his estate,
He begs a share among the swine,
To taste the husks they eat!

2 "I die with hunger here (he cries)
"I starve in foreign lands,
"My father's house has large supplies,
"And bounteous are his hands.

3 "I'll go, and with a mournful tongue
"Fall down before his face,
"Father, I've done thy justice wrong,
"Nor can deserve thy grace."

4 He said, and hasten'd to his home,
To seek his father's love;
The father saw the rebel come,
And all his bowels move.

5 He ran, and fell upon his neck,
Embrac'd and kiss'd his son;
The rebel's heart with sorrow brake
For follies he had done.

6 "Take off his clothes of shame and sin,"
(The father gives command)
"Dress him in garments white and clean,
"With rings adorn his hand.

7 “A day of feasting I ordain,
“Let mirth and joy abound;
“My son was dead, and lives again,
“Was lost, and now is found.”

Hymn 1:124.

The first and second Adam,
Rom.5. 12 &c.

1 Deep in the dust before thy throne
Our guilt and our disgrace we own;
Great God, we own th’ unhappy name
Whence sprang our nature and our shame.

2 Adam, the sinner: At his fall
Death like a conqueror seiz’d us all;
A thousand new-born babes are dead
By fatal union to their head.

3 But whilst our spirits fill’d with awe
Behold the terrors of thy law,
We sing the honours of thy grace,
That sent to save our ruin’d race.

4 We sing thine everlasting Son,
Who join'd our nature to his own;
Adam the second, from the dust
Raises the ruins of the first.

5 [By the rebellion of one man
Thro' all his seed the mischief ran;
And by one man's obedience now
Are all his seed made righteous too.]

6 Where sin did reign, and death abound,
There have the sons of Adam found
Abounding life; there glorious grace
Reigns thro' the Lord our righteousness.

Hymn 1:125.

Christ's compassion to the weak and tempted, Heb. 4. 15 16. and 5. 7. Matt. 12. 20.

1 With joy we meditate the grace
Of our High Priest above;
His heart is made of tenderness,
His bowels melt with love.

2 Touch'd with a sympathy within
He knows our feeble frame;
He knows what sore temptations mean,
For he has felt the same.

3 But spotless, innocent, and pure
The great Redeemer stood,
While Satan's fiery darts he bore,
And did resist to blood.

4 He in the days of feeble flesh
Pour'd out his cries and tears,
And in his measure feels afresh
What every member bears.

5 [He'll never quench the smoking flax,
But raise it to a flame;
The bruised reed he never breaks,
Nor scorns the meanest name.]

6 Then let our humble faith address
His mercy and his power,
We shall obtain delivering grace
In the distressing hour.

Hymn 1:126.

Charity and uncharitableness, Rom. 14. 17 19. 1 Cor. 10. 32.

1 Not different food, or different dress
Compose the kingdom of our Lord,

But peace and joy and righteousness,
Faith and obedience to his word.

2 When weaker Christians we despise
We do the gospel mighty wrong,
For God the gracious and the wise
Receives the feeble with the strong.

3 Let pride and wrath be banish'd hence,
Meekness and love our souls pursue;
Nor shall our practice give offence
To saints, the Gentile or the Jew.

Hymn 1:127.

Christ's invitation to sinners; or,
Humility and pride, Matt. 11. 28 29 30.

1 "Come hither, all ye weary souls,
"Ye heavy laden sinners, come,
"I'll give you rest from all your toils,
"And raise you to my heavenly
home.

2 "They shall find rest that learn of me;
"I'm of a meek and lowly mind;
"But passion rages like the sea,
"And pride is restless as the wind.

3 "Blest is the man whose shoulders take
"My yoke, and bear it with delight;
"My yoke is easy to his neck,
"My grace shall make the burden light."

4 Jesus, we come at thy command,
With faith and hope and humble zeal
Resign our spirits to thy hand,
To mould and guide us at thy will.

Hymn 1:128.

The Apostles' commission; or, The gospel attested by miracles, Mark 16. 15 &c. Matt. 28. 18 &c.

1 "Go preach my gospel, (saith the Lord,)
"Bid the whole earth my grace receive;
"He shall be sav'd that trusts my word,
"He shall be damn'd that won't believe.

2 "[I'll make your great commission known,
"And ye shall prove my gospel true

"By all the works that I have done,
"By all the wonders ye shall do.

3 "Go heal the sick, go raise the dead,
"Go cast out devils in my name;
"Nor let my prophets be afraid,
"Tho' Greeks reproach, and Jews blaspheme.]

4 "Teach all the nations my commands,
"I'm with you till the world shall end;
"All power is trusted to my hands,
"I can destroy, and I defend."

5 He spake, and light shone round his head,
On a bright cloud to heaven he rode;
They to the farthest nations spread
The grace of their ascended God.

Hymn 1:129.

Submission and deliverance; or,
Abraham offering his son, Gen. 22. 6 &c.

1 Saints, at your Father's heavenly word

Give up your comforts to the Lord;
He shall restore what you resign,
Or grant you blessings more divine.

2 So Abraham with obedient hand,
Led forth his son at God's command,
The wood, the fire, the knife he took,
His arm prepar'd the dreadful stroke.

3 "Abraham, forbear, (the angel cry'd)
"Thy faith is known, thy love is try'd,
"Thy son shall live, and in thy seed
"Shall the whole earth be bless'd indeed."

4 Just in the last distressing hour
The Lord displays delivering power;
The mount of danger is the place
Where we shall see surprising grace.

Hymn 1:130.

Love and hatred, Phil. 2. 2. Eph. 4. 30 &c.

1 Now by the bowels of my God,
His sharp distress, his sore complaints,
By his last groans, his dying blood,
I charge my soul to love the saints.

2 Clamour, and wrath, and war be gone,
Envy and spite for ever cease,
Let bitter words no more be known
Amongst the saints, the sons of peace.

3 The Spirit, like a peaceful dove,
Flies from the realms of noise and strife;
Why should we vex and grieve his love,
Who seals our souls to heavenly life?

4 Tender and kind be all our thoughts,
Thro' all our lives let mercy run;
So God forgives our numerous faults
For the clear sake of Christ his Son.

Hymn 1:131.

The Pharisee and the Publican, Luke 18. 10 &c.

1 Behold how sinners disagree,
The Publican and Pharisee!

One doth his righteousness proclaim,
The other owns his guilt and shame.

2 This man at humble distance stands,
And cries for grace with lifted hands;
That boldly rises near the throne,
And talks of duties he has done.

3 The Lord their different language knows,
And different answers he bestows;
The humble soul with grace he crowns,
Whilst on the proud his anger frowns.

4 Dear Father, let me never be
Join'd with the boasting Pharisee;
I have no merits of my own,
But plead the sufferings of thy Son.

Hymn 1:132.

Holiness and grace, Titus 2. 10-13.

1 So let our lips and lives express
The holy gospel we profess,

So let our works and virtues shine
To prove the doctrine all divine.

2 Thus shall we best proclaim abroad
The honours of our saviour God;
When the salvation reigns within,
And grace subdues the power of sin.

3 Our flesh and sense must be deny'd,
Passion and envy, lust and pride;
While justice, temperance, truth and love
Our inward piety approve.

4 Religion bears our spirits up,
While we expect that blessed hope,
The bright appearance of the Lord,
And faith stands leaning on his
word.

Hymn 1:133.

Love and charity, 1 Cor. 13. 2-7 13.

1 Let Pharisees of high esteem
Their faith and zeal declare,
All their religion is a dream
If love be wanting there.

2 Love suffers long with patient eye,
Nor is provok'd in haste;
She lets the present injury die,
And long forgets the past.

3 [Malice and rage, those fires of hell,
She quenches with her tongue;
Hopes, and believes, and thinks
no ill,
Tho' she endure the wrong.]

4 [She nor desires nor seeks to know
The scandals of the time;
Nor looks with pride on those
below,
Nor envies those that climb.]

5 She lays her own advantage by
To seek her neighbour's good;
So God's own Son came down to die,
And bought our lives with blood.

6 Love is the grace that keeps her
power
In all the realms above;
There faith and hope are known no
more,
But saints for ever love.

Hymn 1:134.

Religion vain without love, 1 Cor. 13. 1 2 3.

1 Had I the tongues of Greeks and Jews,
And nobler speech that angels use,
If love be absent, I am found
Like tinkling brass, an empty sound.

2 Were I inspir'd to preach and tell
All that is done in heaven and hell,
Or could my faith the world remove,
Still I am nothing without love.

3 Should I distribute all my store
To feed the bowels of the poor,
Or give my body to the flame
To gain a martyr's glorious name;

4 If love to God and love to men
Be absent, all my hopes are vain;
Nor tongues, nor gifts, nor fiery zeal
The work of love can e'er fulfil.

Hymn 1:135.

The love of Christ shed abroad in the heart, Eph. 3. 16 &c.

1 Come, dearest Lord, descend and dwell
By faith and love in every breast;
Then shall we know, and taste, and feel
The joys that cannot be exprest.

2 Come, fill our hearts with inward strength,
Make our enlarged souls possess,
And learn the height, and breadth, and length
Of thine unmeasurable grace.

3 Now to the God whose power can do
More than our thoughts or wishes know,
Be everlasting honours done
By all the church, thro' Christ his Son.

Hymn 1:136.

Sincerity and hypocrisy; or, Formality in worship, John 4. 24. Psalm 139. 23 24.

1 God is a spirit just and wise,
He sees our inmost mind;
In vain to heaven we raise our cries
And leave our souls behind.

2 Nothing but truth before his throne,
With honour can appear,
The painted hypocrites are known
Thro' the disguise they wear.

3 Their lifted eyes salute the skies,
Their bending knees the ground;
But God abhors the sacrifice
Where not the heart is found.

4 Lord, search my thoughts, and try
my ways,
And make my soul sincere;
Then shall I stand before thy face,
And find acceptance there.

Hymn 1:137.

Salvation by grace in Christ, 2 Tim. 1. 9 10.

1 Now to the power of God supreme
Be everlasting honours given,
He saves from hell, (we bless his Name)
He calls our wandering feet to
heaven.

2 Not for our duties or deserts,
But of his own abounding grace,

He works salvation in our hearts,
And forms a people for his praise.

3 'Twas his own purpose that begun
To rescue rebels doom'd to die;
He gave us grace in Christ his Son
Before he spread the starry sky.

4 Jesus the Lord appears at last,
And makes his Father's counsels
known;
Declares the great transactions past,
And brings immortal blessings down.

5 He dies; and in that dreadful night
Did all the powers of hell destroy;
Rising he brought our heaven to light,
And took possession of the joy.

Hymn 1:138.

Saints in the hands of Christ, John 10. 28 29.

1 Firm as the earth thy gospel stands,
My Lord, my hope, my trust;
If I am found in Jesus' hands,
My soul can ne'er be lost.

2 His honour is engag'd to save
The meanest of his sheep,
All that his heavenly Father gave
His hands securely keep.

3 Nor death, nor hell shall e'er remove
His favourites from his breast;
In the dear bosom of his love
They must for ever rest.

Hymn 1:139.

Hope in the covenant; or, God's promise and truth unchangeable, Heb. 6. 17 18 19.

1 How oft have sin and Satan strove
To rend my soul from thee, my God,
But everlasting is thy love,
And Jesus seals it with his blood.

2 The oath and promise of the Lord
Join to confirm the wondrous grace;
Eternal power performs the word,
And fills all heaven with endless
praise.

3 Amidst temptations sharp and long
My soul to this dear refuge flies:

Hope is my anchor firm and strong,
While tempests blow, and billows rise.

4 The gospel bears my spirits up;
A faithful and unchanging God
Lays the foundation for my hope
In oaths, and promises, and blood.

Hymn 1:140.

A living and a dead faith. Collected from several scriptures.

1 Mistaken souls! that dream of heaven,
And make their empty boast
Of inward joys, and sins forgiven,
While they are slaves to lust.

2 Vain are our fancies airy flights,
If faith be cold and dead,
None but a living power unites
To Christ the living head.

3 'Tis faith that changes all the heart;
'Tis faith that works by love;
That bids all sinful joys depart,
And lifts the thoughts above.

4 'Tis faith that conquers earth and
hell
By a celestial power;
This is the grace that shall prevail
In the decisive hour.

5 [Faith must obey her Father's will
As well as trust his grace;
A pardoning God is jealous still
For his own holiness.

6 When from the curse he sets us free,
He makes our natures clean,
Nor would he send his Son to be
The minister of sin.

7 His Spirit purifies our frame,
And seals our peace with God;
Jesus, and his salvation, came
By water and by blood.]

Hymn 1:141.

The humiliation and exaltation of
Christ, Isa. 53. 1-5 10 11 12.

1 Who has believ'd thy word,
Or thy salvation known?

Reveal thine arm, almighty Lord,
And glorify thy Son.

2 The Jews esteem'd him here
Too mean for their belief:
Sorrows his chief acquaintance
  were,
And his companion, grief.

3 They turn'd their eyes away,
And treated him with scorn;
But 'twas their grief upon him lay,
Their sorrows he has borne.

4 'Twas for the stubborn Jews,
And Gentiles then unknown,
The God of justice pleas'd to bruise
His best beloved Son.

5 "But I'll prolong his days,
"And make his kingdom stand,
"My pleasure, (saith the God of
  grace)
"Shall prosper in his hand.

6 ["His joyful soul shall see
"The purchase of his pain,
"And by his knowledge justify
"The guilty sons of men.]

7 ["Ten thousand captive slaves,
"Releas'd from death and sin,
"Shall quit their prisons and their
graves;
"And own his power divine.]

8 ["Heaven shall advance my Son
"To joys that earth deny'd;
"Who saw the follies men had done,
"And bore their sins, and dy'd."]

Hymn 1:142.

The same, Isa. 53. 6-9 12.

1 Like sheep we went astray,
And broke the fold of God,
Each wandering in a different way,
But all the downward road.

2 How dreadful was the hour
When God our wanderings laid,
And did at once his vengeance pour
Upon the Shepherd's head!

3 How glorious was the grace
When Christ sustain'd the stroke!

His life and blood the Shepherd pays,
A ransom for the flock.

4 His honour and his breath
Were taken both away;
Join'd with the wicked in his death,
And made as vile as they.

5 But God shall raise his head
O'er all the sons of men,
And make him see a numerous seed
To recompense his pain.

6 "I'll give him, (saith the Lord)
"A portion with the strong;
"He shall possess a large reward,
"And hold his honours long."

Hymn 1:143.

Characters of the children of God,
from several scriptures.

1 So new born babes desire the breast
To feed, and grow, and thrive:
So saints with joy the gospel taste,
And by the gospel live.

2 [With inward gust their heart
approves
All that the word relates;
They love the men their Father
loves,
And hate the works he hates.]

3 [Not all the flattering baits on
earth
Can make them slaves to lust;
They can't forget their heavenly
birth,
Nor grovel in the dust.

4 Not all the chains that tyrants use
Shall bind their souls to vice;
Faith like a conqueror can produce
A thousand victories.]

5 [Grace like an uncorrupting seed
Abides and reigns within;
Immortal principles forbid
The sons of God to sin.]

6 [Not by the terrors of a slave
Do they perform his will,
But with the noblest powers they
have
His sweet commands fulfil.]

7 They find access at every hour,
To God within the veil;
Hence they derive a quickening
power,
And joys that never fail.

8 O happy souls! O glorious state
Of overflowing grace!
To dwell so near their Father's seat,
And see his lovely face.

9 Lord, I address thy heavenly throne;
Call me a child of thine,
Send down the Spirit of thy Son
To form my heart divine.

10 There shed thy choicest loves abroad,
And make my comforts strong:
Then shall I say, "My Father God,"
With an unwavering tongue.

Hymn 1:144.

The witnessing and sealing Spirit,
Rom. 8. 14 16. Eph. 1. 13 14.

1 Why should the children of a King
Go mourning all their days?

Great Comforter, descend and bring
Some tokens of thy grace.

2 Dost thou not dwell in all the saints,
And seal the heirs of heaven?
When wilt thou banish my
complaints,
And shew my sins forgiven?

3 Assure my conscience of her part
In the Redeemer's blood;
And bear thy witness with my heart,
That I am born of God.

4 Thou art the earnest of his love,
The pledge of joys to come;
And thy soft wings, celestial dove,
Will safe convey me home.

Hymn 1:145.

Christ and Aaron. Taken from Heb. 7. and 9.

1 Jesus, in thee our eyes behold
A thousand glories more
Than the rich gems and polish'd gold
The sons of Aaron wore.

2 They first their own burnt-offerings
brought
To purge themselves from sin;
Thy life was pure without a spot,
And all thy nature clean.

3 [Fresh blood as constant as the day
Was on their altar spilt;
But thy one offering takes away
For ever all our guilt.]

4 [Their priesthood ran thro' several
hands.
For mortal was their race;
Thy never-changing office stands
Eternal as thy days.]

5 [Once in the circuit of a year
With blood, but not his own,
Aaron within the veil appears
Before the golden throne;

6 But Christ by his own powerful blood
Ascends above the skies,
And in the presence of our God
Shews his own sacrifice.]

7 Jesus, the King of Glory, reigns
On Sion's heavenly hill,

Looks like a lamb that has been slain,
And wears his priesthood still.

8 He ever lives to intercede
Before his Father's face;
Give him, my soul, thy cause to plead,
Nor doubt the Father's grace.

Hymn 1:146.

Characters of Christ, borrowed from inanimate things, in scripture.

1 Go, worship at Immanuel's feet,
See in his face what wonders meet;
Earth is too narrow to express
His worth, his glory, or his grace.

2 [The whole creation can afford
But some faint shadows of my Lord:
Nature to make his beauties known
Must mingle colours not her own.]

3 [Is he compar'd to wine or bread?
Dear Lord, our souls would thus be fed;
That flesh, that dying blood of thine,
Is bread of life, is heavenly wine.]

4 [Is he a tree? The world receives
Salvation from his healing leaves;
That righteous branch, that fruitful
  bough,
Is David's root and offspring too.]

5 [Is he a rose? Not Sharon yields
Such fragrancy in all her fields:
Or if the lily he assume,
The vallies bless the rich perfume.]

6 [Is he a vine? His heavenly root
Supplies the boughs with life and fruit:
O let a lasting union join
My soul the branch to Christ the vine:

7 [Is he the head? Each member lives,
And owns the vital powers he gives;
The saints below, and saints above,
Join'd by his Spirit and his love.]

8 [Is he a fountain? There I bathe,
And heal the plague of sin and death
These waters all my soul renew,
And cleanse my spotted garments
  too.]

9 [Is he a fire? he'll purge my dross,
But the true gold sustains no loss;

Like a refiner shall he sit,
And tread the refuse with his feet.]

10 [Is he a rock? How firm he proves!
The rock of ages never moves;
Yet the sweet streams that from him flow
Attend us all the desert thro'.]

11 [Is he a way? He leads to God,
The path is drawn in lines of blood;
There would I walk with hope and zeal,
Till I arrive at Sion's hill.]

12 [Is he a door? I'll enter in
Behold the pastures large and green,
A paradise divinely fair,
None but the sheep have freedom there.]

13 [Is he design'd a corner-stone,
For men to build their heaven upon?
I'll make him my foundation too,
Nor fear the plots of hell below.]

14 [Is he a temple? I adore
Th'indwelling majesty and power;

And still to this most holy place,
Whene'er I pray, I turn my face.]

15 [Is he a star? He breaks the night,
Piercing the shades with dawning light;
I know his glories from afar,
I know the bright, the morning-star.]

16 [Is he a sun? His beams are grace,
His course is joy, and righteousness;
Nations rejoice when he appears
To chase their clouds, and dry their tears.

17 O let me climb those higher skies,
Where storms and darkness never rise!
There he displays his powers abroad,
And shines, and reigns th'incarnate God.]

18 Nor earth, nor seas, nor sun, nor stars,
Nor heaven his full resemblance bears;
His beauties we can never trace,
Till we behold him face to face.

Hymn 1:147.

The names and titles of Christ, from several scriptures.

1 ['Tis from the treasures
of his word
I borrow titles for my Lord?
Nor art, nor nature can supply
Sufficient forms of majesty.

2 Bright image of the Father's face,
Shining with undiminish'd rays;
Th' eternal God's eternal Son,
The heir, and partner of his
throne.]

3 The King of kings, the Lord most
high,
Writes his own Name upon his thigh:
He wears a garment dipt in blood,
And breaks the nations
with his rod.

4 Where grace can neither melt nor
move
The Lamb resents his injur'd love,
Awakes his wrath without delay,
And Judah's Lion tears the prey.

5 But when for works of peace he comes,
What winning titles he assumes!
“Light of the World, and Life of Men;”
Nor bears those characters in vain.

6 With tender pity in his heart
He acts the Mediator’s part;
A friend and brother he appears,
And well fulfils the names he wears.

7 At length the Judge his throne
ascends,
Divides the rebels from his friends,
And saints in full fruition prove
His rich variety of love.

Hymn 1:148. As the 148th Psalm.

The same.

1 [With cheerful voice I sing
The titles of my Lord,
And borrow all the names
Of honour from his word:
Nature and art
Can ne’er supply
Sufficient forms
Of majesty.

2 In Jesus we behold
His Father's glorious face,
Shining for ever bright
With mild and lovely rays:
Th' eternal God's
Eternal Son
Inherits and
Partakes the throne.]

3 The sovereign King of kings,
The Lord of lords most high,
Writes his own name upon
His garment and his thigh:
His Name is call'd
"The Word of God;"
He rules the earth
With iron rod.

4 Where promises and grace
Can neither melt nor move,
The angry Lamb resents
The injuries of his love;
Awakes his wrath
Without delay,
As lions roar
And tear the prey.

5 But when for works of peace
The great Redeemer comes,

What gentle characters,
What titles he assumes!
"Light of the world,
"And Life of men"
Nor will he bear
Those names in vain.

6 Immense compassion reigns
In our Immanuel's heart,
When he descends to act
A Mediator's part:
He is a friend
And brother too
Divinely kind,
Divinely true.

7 At length the Lord the Judge
His awful throne ascends,
And drives the rebels far
From favourites and friends:
Then shall the saints
Completely prove
The heights and depths
Of all his love.

Hymn 1:149.

The offices of Christ, from several scriptures.

1 Join all the names of love and power
That ever men or angels bore;
All are too mean to speak his worth,
Or set Immanuel's glory forth.

2 But O what condescending ways
He takes to teach his heavenly
grace!
My eyes with joy and wonder see
What forms of love he bears for me.

3 [The "Angel of the covenant" stands
With his commission in his hands,
Sent from his Father's milder
throne,
To make the great
Salvation known.]

4 Great Prophet let me bless thy
Name;
By thee the joyful tidings came,
Of wrath appeas'd, of sins forgiven,
Of hell subdu'd, and peace with
heaven.]

5 [My bright Example, and my Guide,
I would be walking near thy side;
O let me never run astray,
Nor follow the forbidden way!]

6 [I love my Shepherd, he shall keep
My wandering soul among his sheep:
He feeds his flock, he calls their
  names,
And in his bosom bears the lambs.]

7 [My surety undertakes my cause,
Answering his Father's broken laws;
Behold my soul at freedom set;
My surety paid the dreadful debt.]

8 [Jesus, my great High Priest has dy'd,
I seek no sacrifice beside;
His blood did once for all atone,
And now it pleads before the
  throne.]

9 [My advocate appears on high,
The Father lays his thunder by;
Not all that earth or hell can say,
Shall turn my Father's heart away.]

10 [My Lord, my Conqu'ror and my King,
Thy sceptre and thy sword I sing;
Thine is the victory, and I sit
A joyful subject at thy feet.]

11 [Aspire my soul, to glorious deeds,
The "Captain of salvation" leads;

March on, nor fear to win the day,
Tho' death and hell obstruct the way.

12 Should death and hell, and powers unknown
Put all their forms of mischief on,
I shall be safe; for Christ displays
Salvation in more sovereign ways.]

Hymn 1:150. As the 149th Psalm.

The same.

1 Join all the glorious names
Of wisdom, love, and power,
That ever mortals knew,
That angels ever bore:
All are too mean
To speak his worth,
Too mean to set
My Saviour forth.

2 But O what gentle terms,
What condescending ways
Doth our Redeemer use
To teach his heavenly grace!
Mine eyes with joy

And wonder see
What forms of love
He bears for me.

3 [Array'd in mortal flesh
He like an angel stands,
And holds the promises
And pardons in his hands:
Commission'd from
His Father's throne
To make his grace
To mortals known.]

4 [Great Prophet of my God,
My tongue would bless thy Name;
By thee the joyful news
Of our salvation came.
The joyful news
Of sins forgiven,
Of hell subdu'd,
And peace with heaven.]

5 [Be thou my counsellor,
My pattern and my guide,
And thro' this desert land
Still keep me near thy side:
O let my feet
Ne'er run astray,

Nor rove nor seek
The crooked way.]

6 [I love my Shepherd's voice,
His watchful eyes shall keep
My wandering soul among
The thousands of his sheep:
He feeds his flock,
He calls their names,
His bosom bears
The tender lambs.]

7 [To this dear surety's hand
Will I commit my cause;
He answers and fulfils
His Father's broken laws:
Behold my soul
At freedom set!
My surety paid
The dreadful debt.]

8 [Jesus my great high Priest
Offer'd his blood and dy'd;
My guilty conscience seeks
No sacrifice beside:
His powerful blood
Did once atone;
And now it pleads
Before the throne.]

9 [My Advocate appears
For my defence on high,
The Father bows his ear,
And lays his thunder by:
Not all that hell
Or sin can say
Shall turn his heart,
His love away.]

10 [My dear Almighty Lord,
My Conqu'ror and my King,
Thy sceptre and thy sword,
Thy reigning grace I sing:
Thine is the power;
Behold I sit
In willing bonds
Before thy feet.]

11 [Now let my soul arise,
And tread the tempter down
My captain leads me forth
To conquest and a crown.
A feeble saint
Shall win the day,
Tho' death and hell
Obstruct the way.]

12 Should all the hosts of death,
And powers of hell unknown,

Put their most dreadful forms
Of rage and mischief on;
I shall be safe,
For Christ displays
Superior power,
And guardian grace.

END OF THE FIRST BOOK.

Hymns

Book 2
Composed on Divine Subjects

Hymn 2:1.

A song of praise to God from Great Britain.

1 Nature with all her powers shall sing
God the Creator and the King;
Nor air, nor earth, nor skies, nor seas
Deny the tribute of their praise.

2 [Begin to make his glories known,
Ye seraphs that sit near his throne;
Tune your harps high, and spread the sound
To the creation's utmost bound.

3 All mortal things of meaner frame,
Exert your force and own his Name;
Whilst with our souls and with our voice
We sing his honours and our joys.]

4 [To him be sacred all we have
From the young cradle to the grave:
Our lips shall his loud wonders tell,
And every word a miracle.]

5 [This northern isle, our native land,
Lies safe in God th' Almighty's hand:
Our foes of victory dream in vain,
And wear the captivating chain.

6 He builds and guards the British throne,
And makes it gracious like his own,
Makes our successive princes kind,
And gives our dangers to the wind.]

7 Raise monumental praises high
To him that thunders thro' the sky,
And with an awful nod or frown
Shakes an aspiring tyrant down.

8 [Pillars of lasting brass proclaim
The triumphs of th' eternal Name;
While trembling nations read from far
The honours of the God of war.]

9 Thus let our flaming zeal employ
Our loftiest thoughts and loudest songs
Britain pronounce with warmest joy
Hosanna from ten thousand tongues.

10 Yet, mighty God, our feeble frame
Attempts in vain to reach thy Name;
The strongest notes that angels raise
Faint in the worship and the praise.

Hymn 2:2.

The death of a sinner.

1 My thoughts on awful subjects roll,
Damnation and the dead;
What horrors seize the guilty soul
Upon a dying bed!

2 Lingering about these mortal shores,
She makes a long delay,
Till like a flood with rapid force
Death sweeps the wretch away.

3 Then swift and dreadful she descends
Down to the fiery coast,
Amongst abominable fiends,
Herself a frightful ghost.

4 There endless crowds of sinners lie,
And darkness makes their chains;
Tortur'd with keen despair they cry,
Yet wait for fiercer pains.

5 Not all their anguish and their blood
For their old guilt atones,
Nor the compassions of a God
Shall hearken to their groans.

6 Amazing grace, that kept my breath,
Nor bid my soul remove,
Till I had learn'd my Saviour's death,
And well insur'd his love!

Hymn 2:3.

The death and burial of a saint.

1 Why do we mourn departing friends
Or shake at death's alarms?
'Tis but the voice that Jesus sends
To call them to his arms.

2 Are we not tending upward too
As fast as time can move?
Nor would we wish the hours more slow
To keep us from our love.

3 Why should we tremble to convey
Their bodies to the tomb?
There the dear flesh of Jesus lay,
And left a long perfume.

4 The graves of all his saints he bless'd,
And soften'd every bed;
Where should the dying members rest,
But with the dying head?

5 Thence he arose, ascending high,
And shew'd our feet the way;
Up to the Lord our flesh shall fly
At the great rising day.

6 Then let the last loud trumpet sound,
And bid our kindred rise,
Awake, ye nations under ground,
Ye saints, ascend the skies.

Hymn 2:4.

Salvation in the cross.

1 Here at thy cross, my dying God,
I lay my soul beneath thy love,
Beneath the droppings of thy blood,
Jesus, nor shall it e'er remove.

2 Not all that tyrants think or say,
With rage and lightning in their eyes,
Nor hell shall fright my heart away,
Should hell with all its legions rise.

3 Should worlds conspire to drive me thence,
Moveless and firm this heart should lie;
Resolv'd (for that's my last defence)
If I must perish, there to die.

4 But speak, my Lord, and calm my fear,
Am I not safe beneath thy, shade?
Thy vengeance will not strike me here,
Nor Satan dares my soul invade.

5 Yes, I'm secure beneath thy blood,
And all my foes shall lose their aim,
Hosanna to my dying God,
And my best honours to his Name.

Hymn 2:5.

Longing to praise Christ better.

1 Lord, when my thoughts with wonder roll
O'er the sharp sorrows of thy soul,
And read my Maker's broken laws
Repair'd and honour'd by thy cross;

2 When I behold death, hell and sin,
Vanquish'd by that dear blood of thine,

And see the man that groan'd and dy'd
Sit glorious by his Father's side;

3 My passions rise and soar above,
I'm wing'd with faith and fir'd with love;
Fain would I reach eternal things,
And learn the notes that Gabriel sings.

4 But my heart fails, my tongue complains,
For want of their immortal strains;
And in such humble notes as these
Must fall below thy victories.

5 Well, the kind minute must appear
When we shall leave these bodies here,
These clogs of clay, and mount on high,
To join the songs above the sky.

Hymn 2:6.

A morning song.

1 Once more, my soul, the rising day
Salutes thy waking eyes.
Once more, my voice, thy tribute pay
To him that rolls the skies.

2 Night unto night his name repeats,
The day renews the sound,
Wide as the heaven on which he sits
To turn the seasons round.

3 'Tis he supports my mortal frame,
My tongue shall speak his praise;
My sins would rouse his wrath
to flame,
And yet his wrath delays.

4 On a poor worm thy power might
tread,
And I could ne'er withstand;
Thy justice might have crush'd me
dead,
But mercy held thine hand.

5 A thousand wretched souls are fled
Since the last setting sun,
And yet thou length'nest out my
thread,
And yet my moments run.

6 Dear God, let all my hours be thine
Whilst I enjoy the light,
Then shall my sun in smiles decline,
And bring a pleasing night.

Hymn 2:7.

An evening song.

1 [Dread Sovereign, let my evening song
Like holy incense rise;
Assist the offerings of my tongue
To reach the lofty skies.

2 Thro' all the dangers of the day,
Thy hand was still my guard,
And still to drive my wants away
Thy mercy stood prepar'd.]

3 Perpetual blessings from above
Encompass me around,
But O how few returns of love
Hath my Creator found!

4 What have I done for him that dy'd
To save my wretched soul?
How are my follies multiply'd,
Fast as my minutes roll;

5 Lord, with this guilty heart of mine
To thy dear cross I flee,
And to thy grace my soul resign
To be renew'd by thee.

6 Sprinkled afresh with pardoning blood
I lay me down to rest,
As in th' embraces of my God,
Or on my Saviour's breast.

Hymn 2:8.

A hymn for morning or evening.

1 Hosanna, with a cheerful sound,
To God's upholding hand;
Ten thousand snares attend us round,
And yet secure we stand.

2 That was a most amazing power
That rais'd us with a word,
And every day and every hour
We lean upon the Lord.

3 The evening rests our weary head,
And angels guard the room;
We wake and we admire the bed
That was not made our tomb.

4 The rising morning can't assure
That we shall end the day,
For death stands ready at the door
To seize our lives away.

5 Our breath is forfeited by sin
To God's revenging law;
We own thy grace, immortal King,
In every gasp we draw.

6 God is our sun, whose daily light
Our joy and safety brings:
Our feeble flesh lies safe at night
Beneath his shady wings.

Hymn 2:9.

Godly sorrow arising from the sufferings of Christ.

1 Alas! and did my Saviour bleed,
And did my Sovereign die?
Would he devote that sacred head
For such a worm as I?

2 [Thy body slain, sweet Jesus, thine,
And bath'd in its own blood,
While all expos'd to wrath divine
The glorious Sufferer stood.]

3 Was it for crimes that I had done
He groan'd upon the tree?
Amazing pity! grace unknown!
And love beyond degree!

4 Well might the sun in darkness hide,
And shut his glories in,
When God the mighty Maker dy'd
For man the creature's sin.

5 Thus might I hide my blushing face
While his dear cross appears,
Dissolve my heart in thankfulness,
And melt my eyes to tears.

6 But drops of grief can ne'er repay
The debt of love I owe;
Here, Lord, I give myself away,
'Tis all that I can do.

Hymn 2:10.

Parting with carnal joys.

1 My soul forsakes her vain delight,
And bids the world farewell
Base as the dirt beneath my feet,
And mischievous as hell.

2 No longer will I ask your love,
Nor seek your friendship more;
The happiness that I approve
Lies not within your power.

3 There's nothing round this spacious
earth
That suits my large desire;
To boundless joy and solid mirth
My nobler thoughts aspire.

4 [Where pleasure rolls its living flood,
From sin and dross refin'd,
Still springing from the throne
of God,
And fit to cheer the mind.

5 Th' Almighty Ruler of the sphere,
The glorious and the great,
Brings his own all-sufficience there,
To make our bliss complete.]

6 Had I the pinions of a dove,
I'd climb the heavenly road;
There sits my Saviour dress'd in love,
And there my smiling God.

Hymn 2:11.

The same.

1 Send the joys of earth away,
Away ye tempters of the mind,

False as the smooth deceitful sea,
And empty as the whistling wind.

2 Your streams were floating me along
Down to the gulf of black despair,
And whilst I listen'd to your song,
Your streams had e'en convey'd me there.

3 Lord, I adore thy matchless grace,
That warn'd me of that dark abyss,
That drew me from those treacherous seas,
And bid me seek superior bliss.

4 Now to the shining realms above
I stretch my hands, and glance mine eyes;
O for the pinions of a dove
To bear me to the upper skies.

5 There from the bosom of my God
Oceans of endless pleasure roll;
There would I fix my last abode,
And drown the sorrows of my soul.

Hymn 2:12.

Christ is the substance of the Levitical priesthood.

1 The true Messiah now appears,
The types are all withdrawn;
So fly the shadows and the stars
Before the rising dawn.

2 No smoking sweets, nor bleeding lambs,
Nor kid, nor bullock slain,
Incense and spice of costly names
Would all be burnt in vain.

3 Aaron must lay his robes away;
His mitre and his vest,
When God himself comes down to be
The offering and the priest.

4 He took our mortal flesh to show
The wonders of his love;
For us he paid his life below,
And prays for us above.

5 "Father, (he cries) forgive their sins,
"For I myself have dy'd,"
And then he shews his open'd veins,
And pleads his wounded side.

Hymn 2:13.

The creation, preservation, dissolution, and restoration of this world.

1 Sing to the Lord that built the skies,
The Lord that rear'd this stately frame;
Let half the nations sound his praise,
And lands unknown repeat his Name.

2 He form'd the seas, and form'd the hills,
Made every drop and every dust,
Nature and time with all their wheels,
And push'd them into motion first.

3 Now from his high imperial throne
He looks far down upon the spheres;
He bids the shining orbs roll on,
And round he turns our hasty years.

4 Thus shall this moving engine last
Till all his saints are gather'd in,
Then for the trumpet's dreadful blast
To shake it all to dust again!

5 Yet when the sound shall tear the skies,
And lightning burn the globe below,
Saints, you may lift your joyful eyes,
There's a new heaven and earth for you.

Hymn 2:14.

The Lord's day; or, Delight in ordinances.

1 Welcome, sweet day of rest,
That saw the Lord arise;
Welcome to this reviving breast,
And these rejoicing eyes!

2 The King himself comes near,
And feasts his saints to-day,
Here we may sit, and see him here,
And love, and praise, and pray.

3 One day amidst the place
Where my dear God hath been,
Is sweeter than ten thousand days
Of pleasurable sin.

4 My willing soul would stay
In such a frame as this,
And sit and sing herself away
To everlasting bliss.

Hymn 2:15.

The enjoyment of Christ; or, Delight in worship.

1 Far from my thoughts, vain world,
be gone,

Let my religious hours alone;
Fain would my eyes my Saviour see,
I wait a visit, Lord, from thee.

2 My heart grows warm with holy fire,
And kindles with a pure desire:
Come, my dear Jesus, from above,
And feed my soul with heavenly love.

3 [The trees of life immortal stand
In flourishing rows at thy right-hand,
And in sweet murmurs by their side
Rivers of bliss perpetual glide.

4 Haste then, but with a smiling face,
And spread the table of thy grace:
Bring down a taste of fruit divine,
And cheer my heart with sacred wine.]

5 Blest Jesus, what delicious fare!
How sweet thy entertainments are!
Never did angels taste above
Redeeming grace, and dying love.

6 Hail, great Immanuel, all divine,
In thee thy Father's glories shine;
Thou brightest, sweetest, fairest one,
That eyes have seen, or angels
known.

Hymn 2:16.

Part the second.

7 Lord, what a heaven of saving grace,
Shines thro' the beauties of thy
face,
And lights our passions to a flame!
Lord, how we love thy charming
Name!

8 When I can say, my God is mine,
When I can feel thy glories shine,
I tread the world beneath my feet,
And all that earth calls good or
great.

9 While such a scene of sacred joys
Our raptur'd eyes and souls
employs,
Here we could sit, and gaze away
A long, an everlasting day.

10 Well, we shall quickly pass the night
To the fair coasts of perfect light;
Then shall our joyful senses rove
O'er the dear object of our love.

11 [There shall we drink full draughts of bliss,
And pluck new life from heavenly trees:
Yet now, and then, dear Lord, bestow
A drop of heaven on worms below.

12 Send comforts down from thy right-hand,
While we pass thro' this barren land,
And in thy temple let us see
A glimpse of love, a glimpse of thee.]

Hymn 2:17

God's eternity.

1 Rise, rise, my soul, and leave the ground,
Stretch all thy thoughts abroad,
And rouse up every tuneful sound
To praise th' eternal God.

2 Long ere the lofty skies were spread
Jehovah fill'd his throne;

Or Adam form'd, or angels made,
The Maker liv'd alone.

3 His boundless years can ne'er decrease,
But still maintain their prime;
Eternity's his dwelling-place,
And ever is his time.

4 While like a tide our minutes flow,
The present and the past,
He fills his own immortal now,
And sees our ages waste.

5 The sea and sky must perish too,
And vast destruction come!
The creatures—look, how old they grow,
And wait their fiery doom!

6 Well, let the sea shrink all away,
And flame melt down the skies,
My God shall live an endless day,
When th' old creation dies.

Hymn 2:18.

The ministry of angels.

1 High on a hill of dazzling light,
The King of Glory spreads his seat,

And troops of angels stretch'd for flight,
Stand waiting round his awful feet.

2 "Go," saith the Lord, "my Gabriel go,
"Salute the virgin's fruitful womb,[1]
"Make haste, ye cherubs, down below,
Sing and proclaim the Saviour come."

3 Here a bright squadron leaves the skies,
And thick around Elisha stands;[2]
Anon a heavenly soldier flies,
And breaks the chains from Peter's hands.[3]

4 Thy winged troops, O God of hosts,
Wait on thy wandering church below,
Here we are sailing to thy coasts,
Let angels be our convoy too.

---

[1] Luke 1:16.
[2] Luke 2:13.
[3] Acts 11:7.

5 Are they not all thy servants,[4] Lord?
At thy command they go and come
With cheerful haste obey thy word,
And guard thy children to their
home.

Hymn 2:19.

Our frail bodies, and God our preserver.

1 Let others boast how strong they be,
Nor death, nor danger fear;
But we'll confess, O Lord, to thee,
What feeble things we are.

2 Fresh as the grass our bodies stand,
And flourish bright and gay,
A blasting wind sweeps o'er the
land,
And fades the grass away.

3 Our life contains a thousand springs,
And dies if one be gone;
Strange! that a harp of thousand
strings
Should keep in tune so long.

[4] Heb. 1:14.

4 But '.tis our God supports our frame,
The God that built us first;
Salvation to th' Almighty Name,
That rear'd us from the dust.

5 [He spoke, and straight our hearts and brains
In all their motions rose;
"Let blood, (said he) flow round the veins,"
And round the veins it flows.

6 While we have breath, or use our tongues,
Our Maker we'll adore;
His Spirit moves our heaving lungs
Or they would breathe no more.]

Hymn 2:20.

Backslidings and returns; or, The inconstancy of our love.

1 Why is my heart so far from thee,
My God, my chief delight?
Why are my thoughts no more by day
With thee, no more by night?

2 [Why should my foolish passions rove?
Where can such sweetness be
As I have tasted in thy love;
As I have found in thee?]

3 When my forgetful soul renews
The savour of thy grace,
My heart presumes I cannot lose
The relish all my days.

4 But ere one fleeting hour is pass'd,
The flattering world employs
Some sensual bait to seize my taste,
And to pollute my joys.

5 [Trifles of nature or of art
With fair deceitful charms
Intrude upon my thoughtless heart,
And thrust thee from my arms.]

6 Then I repent and vex my soul
That I should leave thee so,
Where will those wild affections roll
That let a Saviour go?

7 [Sin's promis'd joys are turn'd to pain,
And I am drown'd in grief;
But my dear Lord returns again,
He flies to my relief.

8 Seizing my soul with sweet surprise
He draws with loving bands;
Divine compassion in his eyes,
And pardon in his hands.]

9 [Wretch that I am to wander thus
In chase of false delight!
Let me be fasten'd to thy cross,
Rather than lose thy sight.]

10 [Make haste, my days, to reach the goal,
And bring my heart to rest
On the dear centre of my soul,
My God, my Saviour's breast.]

Hymn 2:21.

A song of praise to God the Redeemer.

1 Let the old heathens tune their song
Of great Diana and of Jove;
But the sweet theme that moves my
tongue
Is my Redeemer and his love.

2 Behold a God descends and dies
To save my soul from gaping hell;

How the black gulf where Satan lies
Yawn'd to receive me when I fell!

3 How justice frown'd and vengeance stood
To drive me down to endless pain!
But the great Son propos'd his blood,
And heavenly wrath grew mild again.

4 Infinite lover, gracious Lord,
To thee be endless honours given;
Thy wondrous Name shall be ador'd
Round the wide earth, and wider
heaven.

Hymn 2:22.

With God is terrible majesty.

1 Terrible God, that reign'st on high,
How awful is thy thundering hand!
Thy fiery bolts how fierce they fly!
Nor can all earth or hell withstand.

2 This the old rebel angels knew,
And Satan fell beneath thy frown:
Thine arrows struck the traitor thro',
And weighty vengeance sunk him down.

3 This Sodom felt, and feels it still,
And roars beneath th' eternal load,
"With endless burnings who can dwell,
"Or bear the fury of a God!"

4 Tremble, ye sinners, and submit,
Throw down your arms before his throne,
Bend your heads low beneath his feet,
Or his strong hand shall crush you down.

5 And ye, blest saints, that love him too,
With rev'rence bow before his Name,
Thus all his heavenly servants do:
God is a bright and burning flame.

Hymn 2:23.

The sight of God and Christ in heaven.

1 Descend from heaven, immortal Dove,
Stoop down and take us on thy wings,
And mount and bear us far above
The reach of these inferior things.

2 Beyond, beyond this lower sky,
Up where eternal ages roll,
Where solid pleasures never die,
And fruits immortal feast the soul.

3 O for a sight, a pleasing sight
Of our almighty Father's throne!
There sits our Saviour crown'd with light
Cloth'd in a body like our own.

4 Adoring saints around him stand,
And thrones, and powers before him fall;
The God shines gracious thro' the man,
And sheds sweet glories on them all.

5 O what amazing joys they feel
While to their golden harps they sing,
And sit on every heavenly hill,
And spread the triumphs of their King!

6 When shall the day, dear Lord, appear
That I shall mount to dwell above,
And stand and bow amongst them there,
And view thy face, and sing, and love!

Hymn 2:24.

The evil of sin visible in the fall of angels and men.

1 When the great Builder arch'd the skies,
And form'd all nature with a word,
The joyful cherubs tun'd his praise,
And every bending throne ador'd.

2 High in the midst of all the throng,
Satan, a tall archangel, sat,
Amongst the morning stars he sung [1]
Till sin destroy'd his heavenly state.

3 ['Twas sin that hurl'd him from his throne,
Grov'ling in fire the rebel lies:
"How art thou sunk in darkness down,
"Son of the morning, from the skies!"[2]

4 And thus our two first parents stood
Till sin defil'd the happy place
They lost their garden and their God,
And ruin'd all their unborn race.

---

[1] Job 38:7.
[2] Isaiah 14:12.

5 [So sprung the plague from Adam's
bower,
And spread destruction all abroad;
Sin, the curs'd name, that in one hour
Spoil'd six days labour of a God.]

6 Tremble, my soul, and mourn for grief,
That such a foe should seize thy breast;
Fly to thy Lord for quick relief;
O! may he slay this treacherous guest.

7 Then to thy throne, victorious King,
Then to thy throne our shouts shall rise,
Thine everlasting arm we sing,
For sin the monster bleeds and dies.

Hymn 2:25.

Complaining of spiritual sloth.

1 My drowsy powers, why sleep ye so?
Awake, my sluggish soul!
Nothing has half thy work to do,
Yet nothing's half so dull.

2 The little ants for one poor grain
Labour, and tug, and strive,
Yet we who have a heaven t' obtain,
How negligent we live!

3 We for whose sake all nature stands
And stars their courses move;
We for whose guard the angel bands
Come flying from above;

4 We for whom God the Son came down,
And labour'd for our good,
How careless to secure that crown
He purchas'd with his blood!

5 Lord, shall we lie so sluggish still,
And never act our parts?
Come, holy Dove, from th' heavenly hill,
And sit and warm our hearts.

6 Then shall our active spirits move,
Upward our souls shall rise:
With hands of faith and wings of love
We'll fly and take the prize.

Hymn 2:26.

God invisible.

1 Lord, we are blind, we mortals blind,
We can't behold thy bright abode;

O 'Tis beyond a creature-mind
To glance a thought half-way to God.

2 Infinite leagues beyond the sky
The great Eternal reigns alone,
Where neither wings nor soul
can fly,
Nor angels climb the topless throne.

3 The Lord of glory builds his seat
Of gems insufferably bright,
And lays beneath his sacred feet
Substantial beams of gloomy night.

4 Yet, glorious Lord, thy gracious eyes
Look thro', and cheer us from above;
Beyond our praise thy grandeur
flies,
Yet we adore, and yet we love.

Hymn 2:27.

Praise ye him, all his angels, Psalm 148. 2.

1 God! the eternal awful Name
That the whole heavenly army fears,
That shakes the wide creation's frame,
And Satan trembles when he hears.

2 Like flames of fire his servants are,
And light surrounds his dwelling place;
But, O ye fiery flames, declare
The brighter glories of his face.

3 'Tis not for such poor worms as we
To speak so infinite a thing,
But your immortal eyes survey
The beauties of your sovereign King.

4 Tell how he shews his smiling face,
And clothes all heaven in bright
array;
Triumph and joy run thro' the place,
And songs eternal as the day.

5 Speak, (for you feel his burning love)
What zeal it spreads thro' all your frame:
That sacred fire dwells all above,
For we on earth have lost the name.

6 [Sing of his power and justice too,
That infinite right-hand of his
That vanquish'd Satan and his crew,
And thunder drove them down from
bliss.

7 [What mighty storms of poison'd darts
Were hurl'd upon the rebels there!

What deadly jav'lins nail'd their hearts
Fast to the racks of long despair!]

8 [Shout to your King, you heavenly host,
You that beheld the sinking foe;
Firmly ye stood when they were lost;
Praise the rich grace that kept you so.]

9 Proclaim his wonders from the skies,
Let every distant nation hear;
And while you sound his lofty praise,
Let humble mortals bow and fear.

Hymn 2:28.

Death and eternity.

1 Stoop down, my thoughts, that use to rise,
Converse awhile with death:
Think how a gasping mortal lies,
And pants away his breath.

2 His quivering lip hangs feebly down
His pulses faint and few,
Then, speechless, with a doleful groan
He bids the world adieu.

3 But, O the soul that never dies!
At once it leaves the clay!
Ye thoughts, pursue it where it flies,
And track its wondrous way.

4 Up to the courts where angels dwell,
It mounts triumphing there,
Or devils plunge it down to hell
In infinite despair.

5 And must my body faint and die?
And must this soul remove?
O for some guardian angel nigh
To bear it safe above!

6 Jesus, to thy dear faithful hand
My naked soul I trust,
And my flesh waits for thy
command
To drop into my dust.

Hymn 2:29.

Redemption by price and power.

1 Jesus, with all thy saints above
My tongue would bear her part,
Would sound aloud thy saving love,
And sing thy bleeding heart.

2 Bless'd be the Lamb, my dearest Lord,
Who bought me with his blood,
And quench'd his Father's flaming sword
In his own vital blood:

3 The Lamb that freed my captive soul
From Satan's heavy chains,
And sent the lion down to howl
Where hell and horror reigns.

4 All glory to the dying Lamb,
And never ceasing praise,
While angels live to know his Name,
Or saints to feel his grace.

Hymn 2:30.

Heavenly joy on earth.

1 [Come, we that love the Lord,
And let our joys be known;
Join in a song with sweet accord,
And thus surround the throne.

2 The sorrows of the mind
Be banish'd from the place!
Religion never was design'd
To make our pleasures less.]

3 Let those refuse to sing
That never knew our God,
But favourites of the heavenly King
May speak their joys abroad.

4 [The God that rules on high,
And thunders when he please,
That rides upon the stormy sky
And manages the seas.]

5 This awful God is ours,
Our Father and our love,
He shall send down his heavenly powers
To carry us above.

6 There we shall see his face,
And never, never sin;
There from the rivers of his grace
Drink endless pleasures in.

7 Yes, and before we rise
To that immortal state,
The thoughts of such amazing bliss
Should constant joys create.

8 [The men of grace have found
Glory begun below,
Celestial fruits on earthly ground
From faith and hope may grow.]

9 The hill of Sion yields
A thousand sacred sweets,
Before we reach the heavenly fields,
Or walk the golden streets.

10 Then let our songs abound,
And every tear be dry;
We're marching thro' Immanuel's ground
To fairer worlds on high.

Hymn 2:31.

Christ's presence makes death easy.

1 Why should we start and fear to die?
What timorous worms we mortals are!
Death is the gate of endless joy,
And yet we dread to enter there.

2 The pains, the groans, and dying strife,
Fright our approaching souls away;
Still we shrink back again to life,
Fond of our prison and our clay.

3 O, if my Lord would come and meet,
My soul should stretch her wings in haste,
Fly fearless thro' death's iron gate,
Nor feel the terrors as she pass'd.

4 Jesus can make a dying bed
Feel soft as downy pillows are,
While on his breast I lean my head,
And breathe my life out sweetly there.

Hymn 2:32.

Frailty and Folly.

1 How short and hasty is our life!
How vast our souls' affairs!
Yet senseless mortals vainly strive
To lavish out their years.

2 Our days run thoughtlessly along,
Without a moment's stay;
Just like a story or a song
We pass our lives away.

3 God from on high invites us home,
But we march heedless on,
And ever hastening to the tomb,
Stoop downwards as we run.

4 How we deserve the deepest hell
That slight the joys above!
What chains of vengeance should we feel
That break such cords of love!

5 Draw us, O God, with sovereign grace,
And lift our thoughts on high,
That we may end this mortal race
And see salvation nigh.

Hymn 2:33.

The blessed society in heaven.

1 Raise thee, my soul, fly up, and run
Thro' every heavenly street,
And say, there's nought below the sun
That's worthy of thy feet.

2 [Thus will we mount on sacred wings,
And tread the courts above;
Nor earth, nor all her mightiest things
Shall tempt our meanest love.]

3 There on a high majestic throne
Th' Almighty Father reigns,
And sheds his glorious goodness down
On all the blissful plains.

4 Bright like a sun the Saviour sits,
And spreads eternal noon,
No evenings there, nor gloomy nights,
To want the feeble moon.

5 Amidst those ever-shining skies
Behold the sacred Dove,
While banish'd sin and sorrow flies
From all the realms of love.

6 The glorious tenants of the place
Stand bending round the throne;
And saints and seraphs sing and praise
The infinite Three One.

7 [But O what beams of heavenly grace
Transport them all the while!
Ten thousand smiles from Jesus' face,
And love in every smile!]

8 [Jesus, and when shall that dear day,
That joyful hour appear,
When I shall leave this house of clay
To dwell amongst them there?]

Hymn 2:34.

Breathing after the Holy Spirit;
or, Fervency of devotion desired.

1 Come, holy Spirit, heavenly Dove,
With all thy quickening powers,
Kindle a flame of sacred love,
In these cold hearts of ours.

2 Look, how we grovel here below,
Fond of these trifling toys;
Our souls can neither fly nor go
To reach eternal joys.

3 In vain we tune our formal songs,
In vain we strive to rise;
Hosannas languish on our tongues,
And our devotion dies.

4 Dear Lord! and shall we ever lie
At this poor dying rate?
Our love so faint, so cold to thee,
And thine to us so great?

5 Come holy Spirit, heavenly Dove,
With all thy quickening powers;
Come shed abroad a Saviour's
love,
And that shall kindle ours.

Hymn 2:35.

Praise to God for creation and redemption.

1 Let them neglect thy glory, Lord,
Who never knew thy grace,

But our loud songs shall still record
The wonders of thy praise.

2 We raise our shouts, O God, to thee,
And send them to thy throne,
All glory to th' united Three,
The undivided One.

3 'Twas he (and we'll adore his Name)
That form'd us by a word,
'Tis he restores our ruin'd frame;
Salvation to the Lord.

4 Hosanna! let the earth and skies
Repeat the joyful sound,
Rocks, hills, and vales, reflect the voice
In one eternal round.

Hymn 2:36.

Christ's intercession.

1 Well, the Redeemer's gone
T' appear before our God,
To sprinkle o'er the flaming throne
With his atoning blood.

2 No fiery vengeance now,
Nor burning wrath comes down;
If justice call for sinners' blood,
The Saviour shews his own.

3 Before his Father's eye
Our humble suit he moves,
The Father lays his thunder by,
And looks, and smiles, and loves.

4 Now may our joyful tongues
Our Maker's honour sing,
Jesus the priest receives our songs,
And bears them to the King.

5 [We bow before his face,
And sound his glories high,
"Hosanna to the God of grace
"That lays his thunder by.]

6 "On earth thy mercy reigns,
"And triumphs all above;"
But, Lord how weak are mortal strains
To speak immortal love!

7 [How jarring and how low
Are all the notes we sing!
Sweet Saviour, tune our songs anew,
And they shall please the King.]

Hymn 2:37.

The same.

1 Lift up your eyes to th' heavenly
seats
Where your Redeemer stays;
Kind intercessor, there he sits,
And loves, and pleads, and prays.

2 'Twas well, my soul he dy'd for thee,
And shed his vital blood,
Appeas'd stern justice on the tree,
And then arose to God.

3 Petitions now and praise may rise,
And saints their offerings bring,
The priest with his own sacrifice
Presents them to the King.

4 [Let Papists trust what names they
please,
Their saints and angels boast;
We've no such advocates as these,
Nor pray to th' heavenly host.]

6 Jesus alone shall bear my cries
Up to his Father's throne,
He, dearest Lord! perfumes my sighs,
And sweetens every groan.

6 [Ten thousand praises to the King,
Hosanna in the highest;
Ten thousand thanks our spirits bring
To God and to his Christ.]

Hymn 2:38.

Love to God.

1 Happy the heart where graces reign,
Where love inspires the breast;
Love is the brightest of the train,
And strengthens all the rest.

2 Knowledge, alas! 'Tis all in vain,
And all in vain our fear,
Our stubborn sins will fight and
reign
If love be absent there.

3 'Tis love that makes our cheerful feet
In swift obedience move,
The devils know and tremble too,
But Satan cannot love.

4 This is the grace that lives and sings
When faith and hope shall cease,
'Tis this shall strike our joyful strings
In the sweet realms of bliss.

5 Before we quite forsake our clay,
Or leave this dark abode,
The wings of love bear us away
To see our smiling God.

Hymn 2:39.

he shortness and misery of life.

1 Our days, alas! our mortal days
Are short and wretched too;
"Evil and few," the patriarch says,[1]
And well the patriarch knew.

2 'Tis but at best a narrow bound
That heaven allows to men,
And pains and sins run thro' the round
Of threescore years and ten.

3 Well, if ye must be sad and few,
Run on, my days, in haste;
Moments of sin, and months of woe,
Ye cannot fly too fast.

4 Let heavenly love prepare my soul,
And call her to the skies,

[1] Genesis 47:9.

Where years of long salvation roll,
And glory never dies.

Hymn 2:40.

Our comfort in the covenant made with Christ.

1 Our God, how firm his promise stands,
E'en when he hides his face!
He trusts in our Redeemer's hands
His glory and his grace.

2 Then why, my soul, these sad
complaints,
Since Christ and we are one;
Thy God is faithful to his saints,
Is faithful to his Son.

3 Beneath his smiles my heart has liv'd,
And part of heaven possess'd;
I praise his Name for grace receiv'd,
And trust him for the rest.

Hymn 2:41.

A sight of God mortifies us to the world.

1 [Up to the fields where angels lie,
And living waters gently roll,
Fain would my thoughts leap out
  and fly,
But sin hangs heavy on my soul.

2 Thy wondrous blood, dear dying Christ,
Can make this load of guilt remove;
And thou canst bear me where thou
  fly'st,
On thy kind wings, celestial Dove!]

3 O might I once mount up and see
The glories of th' eternal skies,
What little things these worlds
  would be!
How despicable to my eyes!

4 Had I a glance of thee, my God,
Kingdoms and men would vanish soon,
Vanish, as tho' I saw them not,
As a dim candle dies at noon.

5 Then they might fight, and rage, and
  rave,
I should perceive the noise no more
Than we can hear a shaking leaf,
While rattling thunders round us
  roar.

6 Great All in All, eternal King,
Let me but view thy lovely face,
And all my powers shall bow and sing
Thine endless grandeur and thy
grace.

Hymn 2:42.

Delight in God.

1 My God, what endless pleasures dwell
Above at thy right-hand!
The courts below, how amiable,
Where all thy graces stand!

2 The swallow near thy temple lies,
And chirps a cheerful note;
The lark mounts upward to thy skies,
And tunes her warbling throat:

3 And we, when in thy presence, Lord,
We shout with joyful tongues,
Or sitting round our Father's board,
We crown the feast with songs.

4 While Jesus shines with quickening
grace,
We sing and mount on high;

But if a frown becloud his face,
We faint, and tire, and die.

5 [Just as we see the lonesome dove
Bemoan her widow'd state,
Wandering she flies thro' all the
grove,
And mourns her loving mate.

6 Just so our thoughts from thing to
thing
In restless circles rove,
Just so we drop, and hang the wing,
When Jesus hides his love.]

Hymn 2:43.

Christ's sufferings and glory.

1 Now for a tune of lofty praise
To great Jehovah's equal Son!
Awake, my voice, in heavenly lays,
Tell the loud wonders he hath done.

2 Sing how he left the worlds of light
And the bright robes he wore above,
How swift and joyful was his flight
On wings of everlasting love.

3 Down to this base, this sinful earth
He came to raise our nature high;
He came t' atone almighty wrath;
Jesus the God was born to die.]

4 [Hell and its lions roar'd around,
His precious blood the monsters spilt,
While weighty sorrows press'd him
down,
Large as the loads of all our guilt.]

5 Deep in the shades of gloomy death
Th' almighty Captive pris'ner lay;
Th' almighty Captive left the earth,
And rose to everlasting day.

6 Lift up your eyes, ye sons of light,
Up to his throne of shining grace,
See what immortal glories sit
Round the sweet beauties of his
face.

7 Amongst a thousand harps and
songs
Jesus the God exalted reigns,
His sacred Name fills all their
tongues
And echoes thro' the heavenly
plains!

Hymn 2:44.

Hell; or, The vengeance of God.

1 With holy fear and humble song,
The dreadful God our souls adore;
Reverence and awe becomes the tongue
That speaks the terrors of his power.

2 Far in the deep where darkness dwells,
The land of horror and despair,
Justice has built a dismal hell,
And laid her stores of vengeance there.

3 [Eternal plagues and heavy chains,
Tormenting racks and fiery coals,
And darts t' inflict immortal pains,
Dy'd in the blood of damned souls.]

4 [There Satan the first sinner lies,
And roars, and bites his iron bands;
In vain the rebel strives to rise,
Crush'd with the weight of both thine hands.]

5 There guilty ghosts of Adam's race
Shriek out, and howl beneath thy rod;

Once they could scorn a Saviour's grace,
But they incens'd a dreadful God.

6 Tremble, my soul, and kiss the Son;
Sinners, obey the Saviour's call;
Else your damnation hastens on,
And hell gapes wide to wait your
fall.

Hymn 2:45.

God's condescension to our worship.

1 Thy favours Lord, surprise our souls;
Will the Eternal dwell with us?
What canst thou find beneath the poles
To tempt thy chariot downward thus?

2 Still might he fill his starry throne,
And please his ears with Gabriel's
songs;
But th' heavenly Majesty comes down,
And bows to hearken to our tongues.

3 Great God, what poor returns we pay
For love so infinite as thine!
Words are but air, and tongues but clay,
But thy compassion's all divine.

Hymn 2:46.

God's condescension to human affairs.

1 Up to the Lord that reigns on high,
And views the nations from afar,
Let everlasting praises fly,
And tell how large his bounties are.

2 [He that can shake the worlds he made,
Or with his word, or with his rod,
His goodness how amazing great!
And what a condescending God!]

3 [God that must stoop to view the skies,
And how to see what angels do,
Down to our earth he casts his eyes,
And bends his footsteps downward too.]

4 He over-rules all mortal things,
And manages our mean affairs;
On humble souls the King of kings
Bestows his counsels and his cares.

5 Our sorrows and our tears we pour
Into the bosom of our God,
He hears us in the mournful hour,
And helps us bear the heavy load.

6 In vain might lofty princes try
Such condescension to perform;
For worms were never rais'd so high
Above their meanest fellow-worm.

7 O could our thankful hearts devise
A tribute equal to thy grace,
To the third heaven our songs
should rise,
And teach the golden harps thy praise.

Hymn 2:47.

Glory and grace in the person of Christ.

1 Now to the Lord a noble song!
Awake, my soul, awake, my tongue;
Hosanna to th' eternal Name,
And all his boundless love proclaim.

2 See where it shines in Jesus' face,
The brightest image of his grace;
God, in the person of his Son,
Has all his mightiest works outdone.

3 The spacious earth and spreading
flood
Proclaim the wise, the powerful God;

And thy rich glories from afar
Sparkle in every rolling star.

4 But in his looks a glory stands,
The noblest labour of thine hands:
The pleasing lustre of his eyes
Outshines the wonders of the skies.

5 Grace, 'Tis a sweet, a charming theme;
My thoughts rejoice at Jesus' name:
Ye angels, dwell upon the sound,
Ye heavens, reflect it to the ground!

6 O, may I live to reach the place
Where he unveils his lovely face,
Where all his beauties you behold,
And sing his Name to harps of gold!

Hymn 2:48.

Love to the creatures is dangerous.

1 How vain are all things here below!
How false, and yet how fair!
Each pleasure hath its poison too,
And every sweet a snare.

2 The brightest things below the sky
Give but a flattering light;

We should suspect some danger nigh
Where we possess delight.

3 Our dearest joys, and nearest friends,
The partners of our blood,
How they divide our wavering minds,
And leave but half for God!

4 The fondness of a creature's love,
How strong it strikes the sense!
Thither the warm affections move,
Nor can we call them thence.

5 Dear Saviour, let thy beauties be
My soul's eternal food;
And grace command my heart away
From all created good.

Hymn 2:49.

Moses dying in the embraces of God.

1 Death cannot make our souls afraid
If God be with us there;
We may walk thro' her darkest shade,
And never yield to fear.

2 I could renounce my all below,
If my Creator bid,

And run, if I were call'd to go,
And die as Moses did.

3 Might I but climb to Pisgah's top,
And view the promis'd land,
My flesh itself shall long to drop,
And pray for the command.

4 Clasp'd in my heavenly Father's arms
I would forget my breath,
And lose my life among the charms
Of so divine a death.

Hymn 2:50.

Comfort under sorrows and pains.

1 Now let the Lord my Saviour smile,
And shew my name upon his heart,
I would forget my pains awhile,
And in the pleasure lose the smart.

2 But O it swells my sorrows high
To see my blessed Jesus frown!
My spirits sink, my comforts die,
And all the springs of life are down.

3 Yet why, my soul, why these
complaints?

Still while he frowns his bowels
move;
Still on his heart he bears his saints,
And feels their sorrows and his love.

4 My name is printed on his breast;
His book of life contains my name;
I'd rather have it there impress'd
Than in the bright records of fame.

5 When the last fire burns all things here,
Those letters shall securely stand,
And in the Lamb's fair book appear,
Writ by th' eternal Father's hand.

6 Now shall my minutes smoothly run,
Whil'st here I wait my Father's will;
My rising and my setting sun
Roll gently up and down the hill.

Hymn 2:51.

God the Son equal with the Father.

1 Bright King of Glory, dreadful God!
Our spirits bow before thy seat,
To thee we lift an humble thought,
And worship at thine awful feet.

2 [Thy power hath form'd, thy wisdom
sways
All nature with a sovereign word;
And the bright world of stars obeys
The will of their superior Lord.]

3 [Mercy and truth unite in one,
And smiling sit at thy right-hand;
Eternal justice guards thy throne,
And vengeance waits thy dread
command.]

4 A thousand seraphs strong and
bright
Stand round the glorious Deity;
But who amongst the sons of light
Pretends comparison with thee?

5 Yet there is one of human frame,
Jesus, array'd in flesh and blood,
Thinks it no robbery to claim
A full equality with God.

6 Their glory shines with equal
beams;
Their essence is for ever one,
Tho' they are known by different
names
The Father God, and God the Son.

7 Then let the name of Christ our King
With equal honours be ador'd;
His praise let every angel sing,
And all the nations own their Lord.

Hymn 2:52.

Death dreadful or delightful.

1 Death! 'tis a melancholy day
To those that have no God,
When the poor soul is forc'd away
To seek her last abode.

2 In vain to heaven she lifts her eyes,
But guilt, a heavy chain,
Still drags her downward from the skies
To darkness, fire, and pain.

3 Awake and mourn, ye heirs of hell,
Let stubborn sinners fear,
You must be driven from earth, and dwell
A long for-ever there.

4 See how the pit gapes wide for you,
And flashes in your face,

And thou, my soul, look downwards
  too,
And sing recovering grace.

5 He is a God of sovereign love
That promis'd heaven to me,
And taught my thoughts to soar
  above,
Where happy spirits be.

6 Prepare me, Lord, for thy right-hand,
Then come the joyful day,
Come death, and some celestial band,
To bear my soul away.

Hymn 2:53.

The pilgrimage of the saints; or, Earth and heaven.

1 Lord! what a wretched land is this
That yields us no supply!
No cheering fruits no wholesome trees,
Nor streams of living joy!

2 But pricking thorns thro' all the
  ground
And mortal poisons grow,

And all the rivers that are found
With dangerous waters flow.

3 Yet the clear path to thine abode
Lies thro' this horrid land;
Lord! we would keep the heavenly road,
And run at thy command.

4 [Our souls shall tread the desert thro'
With undiverted feet;
And faith and flaming zeal subdue
The terrors that we meet.]

5 [A thousand savage beasts of prey
Around the forest roam;
But Judah's lion guards the way,
And guides the strangers home.]

6 [Long nights and darkness dwell below,
With scarce a twinkling ray;
But the bright world to which we go
Is everlasting day.]

7 [By glimmering hopes and gloomy fears
We trace the sacred road,

Thro' dismal deeps and dangerous
  snares
We make our way to God.]

8 Our journey is a thorny maze,
But we march upward still;
Forget these troubles of the ways,
And reach at Zion's hill.

9 [See the kind angels at the gates,
Inviting us to come;
There Jesus the fore-runner waits
To welcome travellers home.]

10 There on a green and flowery mount
Our weary souls shall sit,
And with transporting joys recount
The labours of our feet.

11 [No vain discourse shall fill our tongue,
Nor trifles vex our ear,
Infinite grace shall be our song,
And God rejoice to hear.]

12 Eternal glories to the King
That brought us safely thro';
Our tongues shall never cease to
  sing,
And endless praise renew.

Hymn 2:54.

God's presence is light in darkness.

1 My God, the spring of all my joys,
The life of my delights,
The glory of my brightest days,
And comfort of my nights.

2 In darkest shades if he appear,
My dawning is begun;
He is my soul's sweet morning star
And he my rising sun.

3 The opening heavens around me shine
With beams of sacred bliss,
While Jesus shews his heart is mine,
And whispers, "I am his!"

4 My soul would leave this heavy clay
At that transporting word,
Run up with joy the shining way
T' embrace my dearest Lord.

5 Fearless of hell and ghastly death!
I'd break thro' every foe;
The wings of love, and arms of faith
Should bear me conqueror thro'.

Hymn 2:55.

Frail life and succeeding eternity.

1 Thee we adore, eternal Name,
And humbly own to thee,
How feeble is our mortal frame!
What dying worms are we!

2 [Our wasting lives grow shorter still
As months and days increase;
And every beating pulse we tell
Leaves but the number less.

3 The year rolls round, and steals away
The breath that first it gave;
Whate'er we do, where'er we be,
We're travelling to the grave.

4 Dangers stand thick thro' all the ground
To push us to the tomb,
And fierce diseases wait around
To hurry mortals home.

5 Good God! on what a slender thread
Hang everlasting things!
Th' eternal states of all the dead
Upon life's feeble strings.

6 Infinite joy or endless woe
Attends on every breath;
And yet how unconcern'd we go
Upon the brink of death!

7 Waken, O Lord, our drowsy sense
To walk this dangerous road;
And if our souls are hurried hence,
May they be found with God!

Hymn 2:56.

The misery of being without God in this world; or, Vain prosperity.

1 O, I shall envy them no more
Who grow profanely great,
Tho' they increase their golden
store,
And rise to wondrous height.

2 They taste of all the joys that grow
Upon this earthly clod,
Well they may search the creature thro',
For they have ne'er a God.

3 Shake off the thoughts of dying too,
And think your life your own;

But death comes hastening on to you
To mow your glory down.

4 Yes, you must bow your stately head,
Away your spirit flies,
And no kind angel near your bed
To bear it to the skies.

5 Go now, and boast of all your stores,
And tell how bright you shine;
Your heaps of glittering dust are
yours,
And my Redeemer's mine.

Hymn 2:57.

The pleasures of a good conscience.

1 Lord, how secure and bless'd are they
Who feel the joys of pardon'd sin!
Should storms of wrath shake earth
and sea,
Their minds have heaven and peace
within.

2 The day glides sweetly o'er their
heads,
Made up of innocence and love;

And soft and silent as the shades
Their nightly minutes gently move.

3 [Quick as their thoughts their joys come on,
But fly not half so fast away;
Their souls are ever bright as noon,
And calm as summer evenings be.

4 How oft they look to th' heavenly hills,
Where groves of living pleasure grow!
And longing hopes and cheerful smiles
Sit undisturb'd upon their brow.]

5 They scorn to seek our golden toys,
But spend the day and share the night
In numbering o'er the richer joys
That heaven prepares for their delight.

6 While wretched we, like worms and moles,
Lie grovelling in the dust below:
Almighty grace, renew our souls,
And we'll aspire to glory too.

Hymn 2:58

The shortness of life, and the goodness of God.

1 Time! what an empty vapour 'Tis!
And days how swift they are!
Swift as an Indian arrow flies,
Or like a shooting star.

2 [The present moments just appear,
Then slide away in haste,
That we can never say, "They're here,"
But only say, "They're past."]

3 [Our life is ever on the wing,
And death is ever nigh;
The moment when our lives begin
We all begin to die.]

4 Yet, mighty God, our fleeting days
Thy lasting favours share,
Yet with the bounties of thy grace
Thou load'st the rolling year.

5 'Tis sovereign mercy finds us food,
And we are cloth d with love;

While grace stands pointing out the
road
That leads our souls above.

6 His goodness runs an endless round;
All glory to the Lord:
His mercy never knows a bound,
And be his Name ador'd!

7 Thus we begin the lasting song,
And when we close our eyes,
Let the next age thy praise prolong
Till time and nature dies.

Hymn 2:59.

Paradise on earth.

1 Glory to God that walks the sky,
And sends his blessings thro',
That tells his saints of joys on high,
And gives a taste below.

2 [Glory to God that stoops his throne
That dust and worms may see't,
And brings a glimpse of glory down
Around his sacred feet.

3 When Christ, with all his graces
  crown'd,
Sheds his kind beams abroad,
'Tis a young heaven on earthly
  ground,
And glory in the bud.

4 A blooming paradise of joy
In this wild desert springs;
And every sense I straight employ
On sweet celestial things.

5 White lilies all around appear,
And each his glory shows;
The rose of Sharon blossoms here,
The fairest flower that blows.

6 Cheerful I feast on heavenly fruit,
And drink the pleasures down,
Pleasures that flow hard by the foot
Of the eternal throne.]

7 But ah! how soon my joys decay,
How soon my sins arise,
And snatch the heavenly scene away
From these lamenting eyes!

8 When shall the time, dear Jesus, when
The shining day appear,

That I shall leave those clouds of sin,
And guilt and darkness here?

9 Up to the fields above the skies
My hasty feet would go,
There everlasting flowers arise,
And joys unwithering grow.

Hymn 2:60.

The truth of God the promiser; or, The promises are our security.

1 Praise, everlasting praise be paid
To him that earth's foundations laid;
Praise to the God whose strong decrees
Sway the creation as he please.

2 Praise to the goodness of the Lord
Who rules his people by his word,
And there as strong as his decrees
He sets his kindest promises.

3 [Firm are the words his prophets give,
Sweet words on which his children live;

Each of them is the voice of God,
Who spoke and spread the skies
abroad.

4 Each of them powerful as that sound
That bid the new-made heavens go
round;
And stronger than the solid poles,
On which the wheel of nature rolls.]

5 Whence then should doubts and
fears arise,
Why trickling sorrows drown our
eyes?
Slowly, alas, our mind receives
The comforts that our Maker gives.

6 O for a strong, a lasting faith
To credit what th' almighty saith!
T' embrace the message of his Son,
And call the joys of heaven our own.

7 Then should the earth's old pillars shake,
And all the wheels of nature break,
Our steady souls should fear no more
Than solid rocks when billows roar.

8 Our everlasting hopes arise
Above the ruinable skies,

Where the eternal Builder reigns,
And his own courts his power
sustains.

Hymn 2:61.

A thought of death and glory.

1 My soul, come meditate the day,
And think how near it stands,
When thou must quit this house of
clay,
And fly to unknown lands.

2 [And you, mine eyes, look down and
view
The hollow gaping tomb,
This gloomy prison waits for you
Whene'er the summons come.]

3 O could we die with those that die,
And place us in their stead,
Then would our spirits learn to fly,
And converse with the dead:

4 Then should we see the saints
above
In their own glorious forms,

And wonder why our souls should love
To dwell with mortal worms.

5 [How we should scorn these clothes
of flesh,
These fetters and this load!
And long for evening to undress,
That we may rest with God.]

6 We should almost forsake our clay
Before the summons come,
And pray, and wish our souls away
To their eternal home.

Hymn 2:62.

God the thunderer; or, The last judgment and hell.*

1 Sing to the Lord, ye heavenly hosts,
And thou, O earth, adore,
Let death and hell thro' all their coasts,
Stand trembling at his power.

2 His sounding chariot shakes the sky,
He makes the clouds his throne,

* Made in a great sudden storm of thunder, August 20, 1697.

There all his stores of lightning lie,
Till vengeance dart them down.

3 His nostrils breathe out fiery streams,
And from his awful tongue
A sovereign voice divides the flames,
And thunder roars along.

4 Think, O my soul, the dreadful day
When this incensed God
Shall rend the sky, and burn the sea,
And fling his wrath abroad.

5 What shall the wretch the sinner do?
He once defy'd the Lord;
But he shall dread the Thunderer now,
And sink beneath his word.

6 Tempests of angry fire shall roll
To blast the rebel-worm,
And beat upon his naked soul
In one eternal storm.

Hymn 2:63.

A funeral thought.

1 Hark! from the tombs a doleful sound,
My ears attend the cry,

"Ye living men, come view the
ground
"Where you must shortly lie.

2 "Princes, this clay must be your bed,
"In spite of all your towers;
"The tall, the wise, the reverend head
"Must lie as low as ours."

3 Great God, is this our certain doom?
And are we still secure?
Still walking downward to our tomb,
And yet prepare no more?

4 Grant us the powers of quickening
grace
To fit our souls to fly,
Then, when we drop this dying flesh,
We'll rise above the sky.

Hymn 2:64.

God the glory and defence of Sion.

1 Happy the church, thou sacred place,
The seat of thy Creator's grace;
Thine holy courts are his abode,
Thou earthly palace of our God.

2 Thy walls are strength, and at thy
gates
A guard of heavenly warriors waits;
Nor shall thy deep foundations move,
Fix'd on his counsels and his love.

3 Thy foes in vain designs engage,
Against his throne in vain they rage,
Like rising waves, with angry roar,
That dash and die upon the shore.

4 Then let our souls in Zion dwell,
Nor fear the wrath of Rome and hell:
His arms embrace this happy ground,
Like brazen bulwarks built around.

5 God is our shield, and God our sun;
Swift as the fleeting moments run,
On us he sheds new beams of grace,
And we reflect his brightest praise.

Hymn 2:65.

The hope of heaven our support under trials on earth.

1 When I can read my title clear
To mansions in the skies,

I bid farewell to every fear,
And wipe my weeping eyes.

2 Should earth against my soul
engage,
And hellish darts be hurl'd,
Then I can smile at Satan's rage,
And face a frowning world.

3 Let cares like a wild deluge come,
And storms of sorrow fall,
May I but safely reach my home,
My God, my heaven, my all.

4 There shall I bathe my weary soul
In seas of heavenly rest,
And not a wave of trouble roll
Across my peaceful breast.

Hymn 2:66.

A prospect of heaven makes death easy.

1 There is a land of pure delight
Where saints immortal reign,
Infinite day excludes the night,
And pleasures banish pain.

2 There everlasting spring abides,
And never withering flowers:
Death like a narrow sea divides
This heavenly land from ours.

3 [Sweet fields beyond the swelling flood,
Stand dress'd in living green
So to the Jews old Canaan stood,
While Jordan roll'd between.

4 But timorous mortals start and shrink
To cross this narrow sea,
And linger shivering on the brink,
And fear to launch away.]

5 O! could we make our doubts remove,
These gloomy doubts that rise,
And see the Canaan that we love,
With unbeclouded eyes!

6 Could we but climb where Moses stood,
And view the landscape o'er,
Not Jordan's stream, nor death's cold flood,
Should fright us from the shore.

Hymn 2:67.

God's eternal dominion.

1 Great God, how infinite art thou!
What worthless worms are we!
Let the whole race of creatures bow
And pay their praise to thee.

2 Thy throne eternal ages stood,
Ere seas or stars were made;
Thou art the ever-living God
Were all the nations dead.

3 Nature and time quite naked lie
To thine immense survey,
From the formation of the sky
To the great burning day.

4 Eternity with all its years
Stands present in thy view;
To thee there's nothing old appears,
Great God, there's nothing new.

5 Our lives thro' various scenes are drawn,
And vex'd with trifling cares;
While thine eternal thought moves on
Thine undisturb'd affairs.

6 Great God, how infinite art thou!
What worthless worms are we!
Let the whole race of creatures bow
And pay their praise to thee.

Hymn 2:68.

The humble worship of heaven.

1 Father, I long, I faint to see
The place of thine abode,
I'd leave thy earthly courts and flee
Up to thy seat, my God!

2 Here I behold thy distant face,
And 'tis a pleasing sight;
But to abide in thine embrace
Is infinite delight.

3 I'd part with all the joys of sense
To gaze upon thy throne;
Pleasure springs fresh for ever
thence,
Unspeakable, unknown.

4 [There all the heavenly hosts are
seen,
In shining ranks they move,

And drink immortal vigour in,
With wonder and with love.

5 Then at thy feet with awful fear
Th' adoring armies fall
With joy they shrink to *nothing* there,
Before th' Eternal All.

6 There I would vie with all the host
In duty and in bliss,
While *less than nothing* I could boast,
And *vanity* confess.][1]

7 The more thy glories strike mine
eyes,
The humbler I shall lie;
Thus while I sink, my joys shall rise
Unmeasurably high.

Hymn 2:69.

The faithfulness of God in his promises.

1 [Begin, my tongue, some heavenly
theme,
And speak some boundless thing,

[1] Isaiah 40:17.

The mighty works, or mightier name
Of our eternal King.

2 Tell of his wondrous faithfulness,
And sound his power abroad,
Sing the sweet promise of his grace,
And the performing God.

3 Proclaim "salvation from the Lord
"For wretched dying men;"
His hand has writ the sacred word
With an immortal pen.

4 Engrav'd as in eternal brass,
The mighty promise shines;
Nor can the powers of darkness
rase
Those everlasting lines.]

5 [He that can dash whole worlds to
death
And make them when he please,
He speaks, and that almighty breath
Fulfils his great decrees.

6 His very word of grace is strong
As that which built the skies,
The voice that rolls the stars along
Speaks all the promises.

7 He said, "Let the wide heaven be
spread,"
And heaven was stretch'd abroad;
"Abrah'm, I'll be thy God," he said,
And he was Abrah'm's God.

8 O, might I hear thine heavenly
tongue
But whisper, "Thou art mine;"
Those gentle words should raise my
song
To notes almost divine.

9 How would my leaping heart rejoice
And think my heaven secure!
I trust the all-creating voice,
And faith desires no more.]

Hymn 2:70.

God's dominion over the sea,
Psalm 107. 23 &c.

1 God of the seas, thy thundering
voice
Makes all the roaring waves rejoice,
And one soft word of thy command
Can sink them silent in the sand.

2 If but a Moses wave thy rod,
The sea divides, and owns its God:
The stormy floods their Maker knew,
And let his chosen armies thro'.

3 The scaly flocks amidst the sea,
To thee, their Lord, a tribute pay;
The meanest fish that swims the flood
Leaps up, and means a praise to God.

4 [The larger monsters of the deep,
On thy commands attendance keep,
By thy permission sport and play,
And cleave along their foaming way.

5 If God his voice of tempest rears,
Leviathan lies still and fears,
Anon he lifts his nostrils high,
And spouts the ocean to the sky.]

6 How is thy glorious power ador'd,
Amidst those watery nations, Lord!
Yet the bold men that trace the seas,
Bold men, refuse their Maker's praise.

7 [What scenes of miracle they see,
And never tune a song to thee!

While on the flood they safely ride,
They curse the hand that smooths
the tide.

8 Anon they plunge in watery graves,
And some drink death among the
waves:
Yet the surviving crew blaspheme,
Nor own the God that rescu'd them.]

9 O for some signal of thine hand!
Shake all the seas, Lord, shake the
land,
Great Judge, descend, lest men deny
That there's a God that rules the
sky.

From the 70th to the 109th Hymn, I hope the reader will forgive the neglect of the rhyme in the first and third lines of the stanza.

Hymn 2:71.

Praise to God from all creatures.

1 The glories of my Maker God,
My joyful voice shall sing,

And call the nations to adore
Their Former and their King.

2 'Twas his right-hand that shap'd our clay,
And wrought this human frame,
But from his own immediate breath
Our nobler spirits came.

3 We bring our mortal powers to God,
And worship with our tongues:
We claim some kindred with the skies
And join th' angelic songs.

4 Let groveling beasts of every shape,
And fowls of every wing,
And rocks, and trees, and fires, and seas,
Their various tribute bring.

5 Ye planets, to his honour shine,
And wheels of nature roll,
Praise him in your unwearied course
Around the steady pole.

6 The brightness of our Maker's Name
The wide creation fills,
And his unbounded grandeur flies
Beyond the heavenly hills.

Hymn 2:72.

The Lord's Day; or, The resurrection of Christ.

1 Bless'd morning, whose young
  dawning rays
Beheld our rising God,
That saw him triumph o'er the dust,
And leave his dark abode.

2 In the cold prison of a tomb,
The dead Redeemer lay,
Till the revolving skies had brought
The third, th' appointed day.

3 Hell and the grave unite their force
To hold our God in vain,
The sleeping Conqueror arose,
And burst their feeble chain.

4 To thy great Name, Almighty Lord,
These sacred hours we pay,

And loud hosannas shall proclaim
The triumph of the day,

5 [Salvation and immortal praise
To our victorious King,
Let heaven, and earth, and rocks,
  and seas,
With glad hosannas ring.]

Hymn 2:73.

Doubts scattered; or, Spiritual joy restored.

1 Hence from my soul, sad thoughts,
  be gone,
And leave me to my joys,
My tongue shall triumph in my God,
And make a joyful noise.

2 Darkness and doubts had veil'd my
  mind,
And drown'd my head in tears,
Till sovereign grace with shining rays
Dispell'd my gloomy fears.

3 O what immortal joys I felt,
And raptures all divine,

When Jesus told me, I was his,
And my Beloved mine.

4 In vain the tempter frights my soul,
And breaks my peace in vain,
One glimpse, dear Saviour, of thy face,
Revives my joys again.

Hymn 2:74.

Repentance from a sense of divine goodness; or, A complaint of ingratitude.

1 Is this the kind return,
And these the thanks we owe,
Thus to abuse eternal love,
Whence all our blessings flow?

2 TO what a stubborn frame
Has sin reduc'd our mind!
What strange rebellious wretches we,
And God as strangely kind!

3 [On us he bids the sun
Shed his reviving rays,
For us the skies their circles run
To lengthen out our days.

4 The brutes obey their God,
And bow their necks to men,
But we more base, more brutish things
Reject his easy reign.]

5 Turn, turn us, mighty God,
And mould our souls afresh,
Break, sovereign grace, these hearts
  of stone,
And give us hearts of flesh.

6 Let old ingratitude
Provoke our weeping eyes,
And hourly as new mercies fall
Let hourly thanks arise.

Hymn 2:75.

Spiritual and eternal joys; or, The beatific sight of Christ.

1 From thee, my God, my joys shall rise,
And run eternal rounds,
Beyond the limits of the skies
And all created bounds.

2 The holy triumphs of my soul
Shall death itself out-brave,

Leave dull mortality behind,
And fly beyond the grave.

3 There, where my blessed Jesus reigns
In heaven's unmeasur'd space,
I'll spend a long eternity
In pleasure and in praise.

4 Millions of years my wondering eyes
Shall o'er thy beauties rove,
And endless ages I'll adore
The glories of thy love.

5 [Sweet Jesus, every smile of thine
Shall fresh endearments bring,
And thousand tastes of new delight
From all thy graces spring.

6 Haste, my beloved, fetch my soul
Up to thy bless'd abode,
Fly, for my spirit longs to see
My Saviour and my God.

Hymn 2:76.

The resurrection and ascension of Christ.

1 Hosanna to the Prince of Light,
That cloth'd himself in clay,

Enter'd the iron gates of death,
And tore the bars away.

2 Death is no more the king of dread
Since our Immanuel rose,
He took the tyrant's sting away,
And spoil'd our hellish foes.

3 See how the Conqueror mounts
aloft,
And to his Father flies,
With scars of honour in his flesh,
And triumph in his eyes.

4 There our exalted Saviour reigns,
And scatters blessings down,
Our Jesus fills the middle seat
Of the celestial throne.

5 [Raise your devotion, mortal
tongues,
To reach his bless'd abode,
Sweet be the accents of your
songs
To our incarnate God.

6 Bright angels, strike your loudest
strings,
Your sweetest voices raise,

Let heaven, and all created things,
Sound our Immanuel's praise.]

Hymn 77.

The Christian warfare.

1 [Stand up, my soul, shake off thy fears,
And gird the gospel-armour on,
March to the gates of endless joy
Where thy great Captain-Saviour's gone.

2 Hell and thy sins resist thy course,
But hell and sin are vanquish'd foes,
Thy Jesus nail'd them to the cross,
And sung the triumph when he rose.]

3 [What tho' the prince of darkness rage,
And waste the fury of his spite,
Eternal chains confine him down
To fiery deeps, and endless night.

4 'What tho' thine inward lusts rebel,
'Tis but a struggling gasp for life

The weapons of victorious grace
Shall slay thy sins, and end the
strife.]

5 Then let my soul march boldly on,
Press forward to the heavenly gate,
There peace and joy eternal reign,
And glittering robes for conquerors
wait.

6 There shall I wear a starry crown,
And triumph in almighty grace,
While all the armies of the skies
Join in my glorious leader's praise.

Hymn 2:78.

Redemption by Christ.

1 When the first parents of our race
Rebell'd and lost their God,
And the infection of their sin
Had tainted all our blood;

2 Infinite pity touch'd the heart
Of the eternal Son,
Descending from the heavenly court
He left his Father's throne.

3 Aside the Prince of glory threw
His most divine array,
And wrapt his Godhead in a veil
Of our inferior clay.

4 His living power, and dying love
Redeem'd unhappy men,
And rais'd the ruins of our race
To life and God again.

5 To thee, dear Lord, our flesh and soul
We joyfully resign,
Bless'd Jesus, take us for thy own,
For we are doubly thine.

6 Thine honour shall for ever be
The business of our days,
For ever shall our thankful tongue
Speak thy deserved praise.

Hymn 2:79.

Praise to the Redeemer.

1 Plung'd in a gulph of dark despair
We wretched sinners lay,
Without one cheerful beam of hope,
Or spark of glimmering day.

2 With pitying eyes, the Prince of
Grace
Beheld our helpless grief,
He saw, and (O amazing love!)
He ran to our relief.

3 Down from the shining seats
above
With joyful haste he fled,
Enter'd the grave in mortal flesh,
And dwelt among the dead.

4 He spoil'd the Powers of darkness
thus,
And brake our iron chains;
Jesus has freed our captive souls
From everlasting pains.

5 [In vain the baffled prince of hell
His cursed projects tries,
We that were doom'd his endless
slaves,
Are rais'd above the skies.]

6 O for this love, let rocks and hills
Their lasting silence break,
And all harmonious human
tongues
The Saviour's praises speak.

7 [Yes, we will praise thee, dearest Lord,
Our souls are all on flame,
Hosanna round the spacious earth
To thine adored Name.

8 Angels, assist our mighty joys,
Strike all your harps of gold;
But when you raise your highest
notes
His love can ne'er be told.]

Hymn 2:80.

God's awful power and goodness.

1 O the Almighty Lord!
How matchless is his power!
Tremble, O earth, beneath his word,
And all the heavens adore.

2 Let proud imperious kings
Bow low before his throne,
Crouch to his feet, ye haughty
things,
Or he shall tread you down.

3 Above the skies he reigns,
And with amazing blows

He deals unsufferable pains
On his rebellious foes.

4 Yet, everlasting God,
We love to speak thy praise;
Thy sceptre's equal to thy rod,
The sceptre of thy grace.

5 The arms of mighty love
Defend our Sion well,
And heavenly mercy walls us round
From Babylon and hell.

6 Salvation to the King
That sits enthron'd above;
Thus we adore the God of might,
And bless the God of love.

Hymn 2:81.

Our sin the cause of Christ's death.

1 And now the scales have left mine eyes,
Now I begin to see;
O the curs'd deeds my sins have done!
What murderous things they be!

2 Were these the traitors, dearest Lord,
That thy fair body tore?
Monsters, that stain'd those heavenly limbs
With floods of purple gore?

3 Was it for crimes that I had done
My dearest Lord was slain
When justice seiz'd God's only Son,
And put his soul to pain?

4 Forgive my guilt, O Prince of peace,
I'll wound my God no more;
Hence from my heart, ye sins, be gone,
For Jesus I adore.

5 Furnish me, Lord, with heavenly arms
From grace's magazine,
And I'll proclaim eternal war
With every darling sin.

Hymn 2:82.

Redemption and protection from spiritual enemies.

1 Arise my soul, my joyful powers,
And triumph in my God,

Awake, my voice, and loud proclaim
His glorious grace abroad.

2 He rais'd me from the deeps
of sin,
The gates of gaping hell,
And fix'd my standing more secure
Than 'twas before I fell.

3 The arms of everlasting love
Beneath my soul he plac'd,
And on the rock of ages set
My slippery footsteps fast.

4 The city of my bless'd abode
Is wall'd around with grace
Salvation for a bulwark stands
To shield the sacred place.

5 Satan may vent his sharpest
spite,
And all his legions roar,
Almighty mercy guards my life,
And bounds his raging power.

6 Arise, my soul, awake, my voice,
And tunes of pleasure sing,
Loud hallelujahs shall address
My Saviour and my King.

Hymn 2:83.

The passion and exaltation of Christ.

1 Thus saith the Ruler of the skies,
“Awake, my dreadful sword;
“Awake, my wrath and smite the man,
“My fellow,” saith the Lord.

2 Vengeance receiv’d the dread command,
And armed down she flies,
Jesus submits t’ his Father’s hand,
And bows his head and dies.

3 But O! the wisdom and the grace
That join with vengeance now!
He dies to save our guilty race,
And yet he rises too.

4 A person so divine was he
Who yielded to be slain,
That he could give his soul away,
And take his life again.

5 Live, glorious Lord, and reign on high,

Let every nation sing,
And angels sound with endless joy
The Saviour and the King.

Hymn 2:84.

The same.

1 Come, all harmonious tongues,
Your noblest music bring,
'Tis Christ the everlasting God,
And Christ the man we sing.

2 Tell how he took our flesh
To take away our guilt,
Sing the dear drops of sacred blood
That hellish monsters spilt.

3 [Alas, the cruel spear
Went deep into his side,
And the rich flood of purple gore
Their murderous weapons dy'd.]

4 [The waves of swelling grief
Did o'er his bosom roll,
And mountains of almighty wrath
Lay heavy on his soul.]

5 Down to the shades of death
He bow'd his awful head,
Yet he arose to live and reign
When death itself is dead.

6 No more the bloody spear,
The cross and nails no more;
For hell itself shakes at his Name,
And all the heavens adore.

7 There the Redeemer sits
High on the Father's throne;
The Father lays his vengeance by,
And smiles upon his Son.

8 There his full glories shine
With uncreated rays,
And bless his saints' and angels'
eyes
To everlasting days.

Hymn 2:85.

Sufficiency of pardon.

1 Why does your face, ye humble
souls,
Those mournful colours wear?

What doubts are these that waste
  your faith,
And nourish your despair?

2 What tho' your numerous sins
  exceed
The stars that fill the skies,
And aiming at th' eternal throne,
Like pointed mountains rise?

3 What tho' your mighty guilt beyond
The wide creation swell,
And has its curs'd foundations laid
Low as the deeps of hell?

4 See here an endless ocean flows
Of never-failing grace,
Behold a dying Saviour's veins
The sacred flood increase:

5 It rises high and drowns the hills,
'T has neither shore nor bound:
Nor if we search to find our sins,
Our sins can ne'er be found.

6 Awake, our hearts, adore the grace
That buries all our faults,
And pardoning blood that swells above
Our follies and our thoughts.

Hymn 2:86.

Freedom from sin and misery in heaven.

1 Our sins, alas, how strong they be!
And like a violent sea
They break our duty, Lord, to thee,
And hurry us away.

2 The waves of trouble how they rise!
How loud the tempests roar!
But death shall land our weary souls
Safe on the heavenly shore.

3 There to fulfil his sweet commands
Our speedy feet shall move,
No sin shall clog our winged zeal,
Or cool our burning love.

4 There shall we sit, and sing, and tell
The wonders of his grace,
Till heavenly raptures fire our hearts,
And smile in every face.

5 For ever his dear sacred Name
Shall dwell upon our tongue,
And Jesus and salvation be
The close of every song.

Hymn 2:87.

The divine glories above our reason.

1 How wond'rous great, how glorious bright
Must our Creator be,
Who dwells amidst the dazzling light
Of vast infinity!

2 Our soaring spirits upward rise
Tow'rd the celestial throne,
Fain would we see the blessed Three,
And the Almighty One.

3 Our reason stretches all its wings,
And climbs above the skies;
But still how far beneath thy feet
Our groveling reason lies!

4 [Lord, here we bend our humble souls,
And awfully adore,
For the weak pinions of our mind
Can stretch a thought no more.]

5 Thy glories infinitely rise
Above our labouring tongue;

In vain the highest seraph tries
To form an equal song.

6 [In humble notes our faith adores
The great mysterious King,
While angels strain their nobler
powers,
And sweep th' immortal string.]

Hymn 2:88.

Salvation.

1 Salvation! O, the joyful sound!
'Tis pleasure to our ears;
A sovereign balm for every
wound,
A cordial for our fears.

2 Buried in sorrow and in sin,
At hell's dark door we lay,
But we arise by grace divine
To see a heavenly day.

3 Salvation! let the echo fly
The spacious earth around,
While all the armies of the sky
Conspire to raise the sound.

Hymn 2:89.

Christ's victory over Satan.

1 Hosanna to our conquering King!
The prince of darkness flies,
His troops rush headlong down to hell
Like lightning from the skies.

2 There, bound in chains, the lions roar,
And fright the rescu'd sheep,
But heavy bars confine their power
And malice to the deep.

3 Hosanna to our conquering King,
All hail, incarnate love!
Ten thousand songs and glories wait
To crown thy head above.

4 Thy victories and thy deathless fame
Thro' the wide world shall run,
And everlasting ages sing
The triumphs thou hast won.

Hymn 2:90.

Faith in Christ for pardon and sanctification.

1 How sad our state by nature is!
Our sin how deep it stains!
And Satan binds our captive minds
Fast in his slavish chains.

2 But there's a voice of sovereign grace
Sounds from the sacred word,
"Ho, ye despairing sinners, come,
"And trust upon the Lord."

3 My soul obeys th' almighty call,
And runs to this relief,
I would believe thy promise, Lord,
O! help my unbelief.

4 [To the dear fountain of thy blood,
Incarnate God, I fly,
Here let me wash my spotted soul
From crimes of deepest die.

5 Stretch out thine arm victorious King,
My reigning sins subdue,
Drive the old dragon from his seat,
With all his hellish crew.]

6 A guilty, weak, and helpless worm,
On thy kind arms I fall:
Be thou my strength and righteousness,
My Jesus, and my all.

Hymn 2:91.

The glory of Christ in heaven.

1 O the delights, the heavenly joys,
The glories of the place
Where Jesus sheds the brightest beams
Of his o'erflowing grace.

2 Sweet majesty and awful love
Sit smiling on his brow,
And all the glorious ranks above
At humble distance bow.

3 [Princes to his imperial Name
Bend their bright sceptres down,
Dominions, thrones, and powers
rejoice
To see him wear the crown.]

4 Archangels sound his lofty praise
Thro' every heavenly street,
And lay their highest honours down
Submissive at his feet.

5 Those soft, those blessed feet of his
That once rude iron tore,
High on a throne of light they stand,
And all the saints adore.

6 His head, the dear majestic head
That cruel thorns did wound,
See what immortal glories shine,
And circle it around.

7 This is the Man, th' exalted Man,
Whom we unseen adore;
But when our eyes behold his face,
Our hearts shall love him more.

8 [Lord, how our souls are all on fire
To see thy bless'd abode,
Our tongues rejoice in tunes of
praise
To our incarnate God.

9 And whilst our faith enjoys this
sight,
We long to leave our clay,
And wish thy fiery chariots, Lord,
To fetch our souls away.]

Hymn 2:92

The church saved, and her enemies disappointed.

Composed the 5th of November, 1694.

1 Shout to the Lord, and let our joys
Thro' the whole nation run;
Ye British skies, resound the noise
Beyond the rising sun.

2 Thee, mighty God, our souls admire,
Thee our glad voices sing,
And join with the celestial choir
To praise th' eternal King.

3 Thy power the whole creation rules,
And on the starry skies
Sits smiling at the weak designs
Thine envious foes devise.

4 Thy scorn derides their feeble rage,
And with an awful frown
Flings vast confusion on their plots,
And shakes their Babel down.

5 [Their secret fires in caverns lay,
And we the sacrifice:
But gloomy caverns strove in vain
To 'scape all-searching eyes.

6 Their dark designs were all reveal'd,
Their treasons all betray'd:
Praise to the God that broke the snare
Their cursed hands had laid.]

7 In vain the busy sons of hell
Still new rebellions try,
Their souls shall pine with envious rage,
And vex away and die.

8 Almighty grace defends our land
From their malicious power,
Let Britain with united songs
Almighty grace adore.

Hymn 2:93.

God all, and in all, Psalm 73. 25.

1 My God, my life, my love,
To thee, to thee I call,
I cannot live if thou remove,
For thou art all in all.

2 [Thy shining grace can cheer,
This dungeon where I dwell;
'Tis paradise when thou art here;
If thou depart, 'Tis hell.]

3 [The smilings of thy face,
How amiable they are!
'Tis heaven to rest in thine embrace,
And no where else but there.]

4 [To thee, and thee alone,
The angels owe their bliss;
They sit around thy gracious throne,
And dwell where Jesus is.]

5 [Not all the harps above
Can make a heavenly place,
If God his residence remove,
Or but conceal his face.]

6 Nor earth nor all the sky
Can one delight afford;
No not a drop of real joy,
Without thy presence, Lord.

7 Thou art the sea of love,
Where all my pleasures roll,
The circle where my passions move,
And centre of my soul.

8 [To thee my spirits fly
With infinite desire;
And yet how far from thee I lie!
Dear Jesus, raise me higher!]

Hymn 2:94.

God my only happiness, Psalm 73. 25.

1 My God, my portion, and my love,
My everlasting all,
I've none but thee in heaven above,
Or on this earthly ball.

2 [What empty things are all the skies,
And this inferior clod!
There's nothing here deserves my joys,
There's nothing like my God.]

3 [In vain the bright, the burning sun
Scatters his feeble light;
'Tis thy sweet beams create my noon;
If thou withdraw, 'Tis night.

4 And whilst upon my restless bed,
Amongst the shades I roll,
If my Redeemer shew his head
'Tis morning with my soul.]

5 To thee we owe our wealth and friends,
And health, and safe abode;
Thanks to thy Name for meaner things,
But they are not my God.

6 How vain a toy is glittering wealth,
If once compar'd to thee;
Or what's my safety, or my health,
Or all my friends to me?

7 Were I possessor of the earth,
And call'd the stars my own
Without thy graces and thyself
I were a wretch undone.

8 Let others stretch their arms like seas,
And grasp in all the shore,
Grant me the visits of thy face,
And I desire no more.

Hymn 2:95.

Look on him whom they pierced, and mourn.

1 Infinite grief! amazing woe!
Behold my bleeding Lord:
Hell and the Jews conspir'd his death,
And us'd the Roman sword.

2 O the sharp pangs of smarting pain
My dear Redeemer bore,
When knotty whips and ragged thorns
His sacred body tore!

3 But knotty whips and ragged thorns
In vain do I accuse;

In vain I blame the Roman bands,
And the more spiteful Jews.

4 'Twere you, my sins, my cruel sins,
His chief tormentors were;
Each of my crimes became a nail,
And unbelief the spear.

5 'Twere you that pull'd the vengeance down
Upon his guiltless head:
Break, break, my heart, O burst mine eyes!
And let my sorrows bleed.

6 Strike, mighty grace, my flinty soul,
Till melting waters flow,
And deep repentance drown mine eyes
In undissembled woe.

Hymn 2:96.

Distinguishing love; or, Angels punished and men saved.

1 Down headlong from their native skies

The rebel angels fell,
And thunderbolts of flaming wrath
Pursu'd them deep to hell.

2 Down from the top of earthly bliss
Rebellious man was hurl'd
And Jesus stoop'd beneath the grave
To reach a sinking world.

3 O love of infinite degree!
Unmeasurable grace!
Must heaven's eternal Darling die
To save a traitorous race?

4 Must angels sink for ever down,
And burn in quenchless fire,
While God forsakes his shining
  throne
To raise us wretches higher?

5 O for this love let earth and skies
With hallelujahs ring,
And the full choir of human tongues
All hallelujah sing.

Hymn 2:97.

The same.

1 From heaven the sinning angels fell,
And wrath and darkness chain'd
them down;
But man, vile man, forsook his bliss,
And mercy lifts him to a crown.

2 Amazing work of sovereign grace
That could distinguish rebels so!
Our guilty treasons call'd aloud
For everlasting fetters too.

3 To thee, to thee, Almighty Love,
Our souls, ourselves, our all we pay:
Millions of tongues shall sound thy
praise
On the bright hills of heavenly day.

Hymn 2:98.

Hardness of heart complained of.

1 My heart, how dreadful hard it is!
How heavy here it lies,
Heavy and cold within my breast
Just like a rock of ice!

2 Sin like a raging tyrant sits
Upon this flinty throne,

And every grace lies buried deep
Beneath this heart of stone.

3 How seldom do I rise to God,
Or taste the joys above!
This mountain presses down my faith,
And chills my flaming love.

4 When smiling mercy courts my soul
With all its heavenly charms,
This stubborn, this relentless thing
Would thrust it from my arms.

5 Against the thunders of thy word
Rebellious I have stood,
My heart it shakes not at the wrath
And terrors of a God.

6 Dear Saviour, steep this rock of mine
In thine own crimson sea:
None but a bath of blood divine
Can melt the flint away.

Hymn 2:99.

The book of God's decrees.

1 Let the whole race of creatures lie
Abas'd before their God;

Whate'er his sovereign voice hath
form'd
He governs with a nod.

2 [Ten thousand ages ere the skies
Were into motion brought,
All the long years and worlds to
come
Stood present to his thought.]

5 [There's not a sparrow or a worm
But's found in his decrees;
He raises monarchs to their thrones,
And sinks them as he please.]

4 If light attends the course I run,
'Tis he provides those rays;
And 'Tis his hand that hides my sun,
If darkness cloud my days.

5 Yet I would not be much concern'd,
Nor vainly long to see
The volume of his deep decrees,
What months are writ for me.

6 When he reveals the book of life,
O, may I read my name
Amongst the chosen of his love,
The followers of the Lamb!

Hymn 2:100.

The presence of Christ is the life of my soul.

1 [How full of anguish is the thought,
How it distracts and tears my heart
If God, at last, my sovereign Judge,
Should frown, and bid my soul, "Depart!"]

2 Lord, when I quit this earthly stage,
Where shall I fly but to thy breast?
For I have sought no other home
For I have learn'd no other rest.

3 I cannot live contented here,
Without some glimpses of thy face;
And heaven without thy presence there
Would be a dark and tiresome place.

4 When earthly cares engross the day
And hold my thoughts aside from thee,
The shining hours of cheerful light
Are long and tedious years to me.

5 And if no evening visit's paid
Between my Saviour and my soul,
How dull the night! how sad the
shade!
How mournfully the minutes roll!

6 This flesh of mine might learn as soon
To live, yet part with all my blood;
To breathe when vital air is gone,
Or thrive and grow without my food.

7 [Christ is my light, my life, my care,
My blessed hope, my heavenly prize,
Dearer than all my passions are,
My limbs, my bowels, or my eyes.

8 The strings that twine about my heart,
Tortures and racks may tear them off,
But they can never, never part
With their dear hold of Christ my
love.]

9 [My God! and can an humble child
That loves thee with a flame so high,
Be ever from thy face exil'd
Without the pity of thine eye?

10 Impossible—For thine own hands
Have tied my heart so fast to thee;

And in thy book the promise stands,
That where thou art thy friends
 must be.

Hymn 2:101.

The world's three great temptations.

1 When in the light of faith divine
We look on things below,
Honour, and gold, and sensual joy,
How vain and dangerous too!

2 [Honour's a puff of noisy breath;
Yet men expose their blood,
And venture everlasting death
To gain that airy good.

3 Whilst others starve the nobler mind,
And feed on shining dust,
They rob the serpent of his food
T' indulge a sordid lust.]

4 The pleasures that allure our sense
Are dangerous snares to souls;
There's but a drop of flattering
 sweet,
And dash'd with bitter bowls.

5 God is mine all-sufficient good,
My portion and my choice;
In him my vast desires are fill'd,
And all my powers rejoice.

6 In vain the world accosts my ear,
And tempts my heart anew;
I cannot buy your bliss so dear,
Nor part with heaven for you.

Hymn 2:102.

A happy resurrection.

1 No, I'll repine at death no more,
But with a cheerful gasp resign
To the cold dungeon of the grave
These dying, withering limbs of
mine.

2 Let worms devour my wasting flesh,
And crumble all my bones to dust,
My God shall raise my frame anew
At the revival of the just.

3 Break, sacred morning, thro' the
skies,
Bring that delightful, dreadful day,

Cut short the hours, dear Lord, and
come,
Thy lingering wheels, how long they
stay!

4 [Our weary spirits faint to see
The light of thy returning face,
And hear the language of those lips
Where God has shed his richest grace.]

5 Haste then upon the wings of love,
Rouse all the pious sleeping clay,
That we may join in heavenly joys,
And sing the triumph of the day.

Hymn 2:103.

Christ's commission, John 3. 16 17.

1 Come happy souls, approach your God
With new melodious songs;
Come, render to almighty grace
The tribute of your tongues.

2 So strange, so boundless was the love
That pity'd dying men,
The Father sent his equal Son
To give them life again.

3 Thy hands, dear Jesus, were not
  arm'd
With a revenging rod,
No hard commission to perform
The vengeance of a God.

4 But all was mercy, all was mild,
And wrath forsook the throne,
When Christ on the kind errand came,
And brought salvation down.

5 Here, sinners, you may heal your
  wounds,
And wipe your sorrows dry;
Trust in the mighty Saviour's Name,
And you shall never die.

6 See, dearest Lord our willing souls
Accept thine offer'd grace;
We bless the great Redeemer's love,
And give the Father praise.

Hymn 2:104.

The same.

1 Raise your triumphant songs
To an immortal tune,

Let the wide earth resound the
  deeds
Celestial grace has done.

2 Sing how eternal love
Its chief beloved chose,
And bid him raise our wretched race
From their abyss of woes.

3 His hand no thunder bears,
Nor terror clothes his brow,
No bolts to drive our guilty souls
To fiercer flames below.

4 'Twas mercy fill'd the throne,
And wrath stood silent by,
When Christ was sent with pardons
  down
To rebels doom'd to die.

5 Now, sinners, dry your tears,
Let hopeless sorrow cease;
Bow to the sceptre of his love,
And take the offer'd peace.

6 Lord we obey thy call;
We lay an humble claim
To the salvation thou hast brought,
And love and praise thy Name.

Hymn 2:105.

Repentance flowing from the patience of God.

1 And are we wretches yet alive?
And do we yet rebel?
'Tis boundless, 'Tis amazing love
That bears us up from hell!

2 The burden of our weighty guilt
Would sink us down to flames,
And threatening vengeance rolls
above
To crush our feeble frames.

3 Almighty goodness cries, "Forbear;"
And straight the thunder stays;
And dare we now provoke his wrath,
And weary out his grace?

4 Lord, we have long abus'd thy love,
Too long indulg'd our sin;
Our aching hearts e'en bleed to see
What rebels we have been.

5 No more, ye lusts, shall ye
command,
No more will we obey;

Stretch out, O God, thy conquering
hand,
And drive thy foes away.

Hymn 2:106.

Repentance at the cross.

1 Oh, if my soul was form'd for woe,
How would I vent my sighs!
Repentance should like rivers flow
From both my streaming eyes.

2 'Twas for my sins, my dearest Lord
Hung on the cursed tree,
And groan'd away a dying life,
For thee, my soul, for thee.

3 O how I hate those lusts of mine
That crucify'd my God,
Those sins that pierc'd and nail'd his
flesh
Fast to the fatal wood!

4 Yes, my Redeemer, they shall die,
My heart has so decreed,
Nor will I spare the guilty things
That made my Saviour bleed.

5 Whilst with a melting broken heart
My murder'd Lord I view,
I'll raise revenge against my sins,
And slay the murderers too.

Hymn 2:107.

The everlasting absence of God intolerable.

1 That awful day will surely come,
Th' appointed hour makes haste,
When I must stand before my
Judge,
And pass the solemn test.

2 Thou lovely chief of all my joys,
Thou sovereign of my heart,
How could I bear to hear thy voice
Pronounce the sound, "Depart?"

3 [The thunder of that dismal word,
Would so torment my ear,
'Twould tear my soul asunder, Lord,
With most tormenting fear.]

4 [What, to be banish'd from my life,
And yet forbid to die!

To linger in eternal pain,
Yet death for ever fly!]

5 O wretched state of deep despair,
To see my God remove,
And fix my doleful station where
I must not taste his Love.

6 Jesus, I throw my arms around,
And hang upon thy breast;
Without a gracious smile from thee
My spirit cannot rest.

7 O tell me that my worthless name
Is graven on thy hands;
Shew me some promise in thy book
Where my salvation stands!

8 [Give me one kind assuring word,
To sink my fears again,
And cheerfully my soul shall wait
Her threescore years and ten.]

Hymn 2:108.

Access to the throne of grace by a Mediator.

1 Come, let us lift our joyful eyes
Up to the courts above,

And smile to see our Father there
Upon a throne of love.

2 Once ‘twas a seat of dreadful wrath,
And shot devouring flame;
Our God appear’d consuming fire,
And vengeance was his name.

3 Rich were the drops of Jesus’ blood,
That calm’d his frowning face,
That sprinkled o’er the burning
throne,
And turn’d the wrath to grace.

4 Now we may bow before his feet,
And venture near the Lord;
No fiery cherub guards his seat,
Nor double-flaming sword.

5 The peaceful gates of heavenly bliss
Are open’d by the Son;
High let us raise our notes of praise,
And reach th’ Almighty throne.

6 To thee ten thousand thanks we
bring
Great Advocate on high:
And glory to th’ eternal King
That lays his fury by.

Hymn 2:109.

The darkness of providence.

1 Lord, we adore thy vast designs,
Th' obscure abyss of providence,
Too deep to sound with mortal lines
Too dark to view with feeble sense.

2 Now thou array'st thine awful face
In angry frowns, without a smile;
We thro' the cloud believe thy grace,
Secure of thy compassion still.

3 Thro' seas and storms of deep distress
We sail by faith and not by sight;
Faith guides us in the wilderness
Through all the briers and the night.

4 Dear Father, if thy lifted rod
Resolve to scourge us here below,
Still we must lean upon our God,
Thine arm shall bear us safely thro'.

Hymn 2:110.

Triumph over death in hope of the resurrection.

1 And must this body die?
This mortal frame decay?
And must these active limbs of mine
Lie mouldering in the clay?

2 Corruption, earth and worms,
Shall but refine this flesh,
Till my triumphant spirit comes
To put it on afresh.

3 God my Redeemer lives,
And often from the skies
Looks down, and watches all my dust,
Till he shall bid it rise.

4 Array'd in glorious grace
Shall these vile bodies shine,
And every shape and every face
Look heavenly and divine.

5 These lively hopes we owe
To Jesus' dying love;
We would adore his grace below,
And sing his power above.

6 Dear Lord, accept the praise
Of these our humble songs,
Till tunes of nobler sound we raise
With our immortal tongues.

Hymn 2:111.

Thanksgiving for victory; or, God's dominion and our deliverance.

1 Zion rejoice, and Judah sing;
The Lord assumes his throne;
Let Britain own the heavenly King,
And make his glories known.

2 The great, the wicked, and the
proud,
From their high seats are hurl'd;
Jehovah rides upon a cloud,
And thunders thro' the world.

3 He reigns upon th' eternal hills,
Distributes mortal crowns,
Empires are fix'd beneath his smiles,
And totter at his frowns.

4 Navies, that rule the ocean wide,
Are vanquish'd by his breath;
And legions arm'd with power and
pride
Descend to watery death.

5 Let tyrants make no more pretence
To vex our happy land;

Jehovah's Name is our defence,
Our buckler is his hand.

6 [Long may the King our Sovereign live
To rule us by his word;
And all the honours he can give
Be offer'd to the Lord.]

Hymn 2:112.

Angels ministering to Christ and saints.

1 Great God, to what a glorious height
Hast thou advanc'd the Lord thy Son!
Angels, in all their robes of light,
Are made the servants of his throne.

2 Before his feet their armies wait,
And swift as flames of fire they move,
To manage his affairs of state
In works of vengeance or of love.

3 His orders run thro' all their hosts,
Legions descend at his command
To shield and guard the British coasts,
When foreign rage invades our land.

4 Now they are sent to guide our feet
Up to the gates of thine abode,
Thro' all the dangers that we meet
In travelling the heavenly road.

5 Lord, when I leave this mortal
ground,
And thou shall bid me rise and
come,
Send a beloved angel down
Safe to conduct my spirit home.

Hymn 2:113.

The same.

1 The majesty of Solomon!
How glorious to behold
The servants waiting round his throne,
The ivory and the gold.

2 But, mighty God, thy palace shines
With far superior beams;
Thine angel-guards are swift as winds,
Thy ministers are flames.

3 [Soon as thine only Son had made
His entrance on this earth,

A shining army downward fled
To celebrate his birth.

4 And when oppress'd with pains and
 fears
On the cold ground he lies,
Behold a heavenly form appears
T' allay his agonies.]

5 Now to the hands of Christ our King
Are all their legions given;
They wait upon his saints, and bring
His chosen heirs to heaven.

6 Pleasure and praise run thro' their
 host
To see a sinner turn;
Then Satan has a captive lost,
And Christ a subject born.

7 But there's an hour of brighter joy,
When he his angels sends
Obstinate rebels to destroy,
And gather in his friends.

8 O! could I say, without a doubt,
There shall my soul be found,
Then let the great archangel shout,
And the last trumpet sound.

Hymn 2:114.

Christ's death, victory and dominion.

1 I sing my Saviour's wondrous death;
He conquer'd when he fell:
'*Tis finish'd*, said his dying breath,
And shook the gates of hell.

2 '*Tis finish'd*, our Immanuel cries,
The dreadful work is done;
Hence shall his sovereign throne
arise,
His kingdom is begun.

3 His cross a sure foundation laid
For glory and renown,
When thro' the regions of the dead
He pass'd to reach the crown.

4 Exalted at his Father's side
Sits our victorious Lord;
To heaven and hell his hands divide
The vengeance or reward.

5 The saints from his propitious eye
Await their several crowns,
And all the sons of darkness fly
The terror of his frowns.

Hymn 2:115.

God the avenger of his saints; or, His kingdom.

1 High as the heavens above the ground
Reigns the Creator God;
Wide as the whole creation's bound
Extends his awful rod.

2 Let princes of exalted state
To him ascribe their crown,
Render their homage at his feet,
And cast their glories down.

3 Know that his kingdom is supreme,
Your lofty thoughts are vain;
He calls you gods, that awful name,
But ye must die like men.

4 Then let the sovereigns of the globe
Not dare to vex the just;
He puts on vengeance like a robe,
And treads the worms to dust.

5 Ye judges of the earth, be wise,
And think on heaven with fear;
The meanest saint that you despise
Has an avenger there.

Hymn 2:116.

Mercies and thanks.

1 How can I sink with such a prop
As my eternal God,
Who bears the earth's huge pillars
up,
And spreads the heavens abroad?

2 How can I die while Jesus lives,
Who rose and left the dead?
Pardon and grace my soul receives
From mine exalted head.

3 All that I am, and all I have
Shall be for ever thine,
Whate'er my duty bids me give
My cheerful hands resign.

4 Yet if I might make some reserve,
And duty did not call,
I love my God with zeal so great
That I should give him all.

Hymn 2:117.

Living and dying with God present.

1 I cannot bear thine absence, Lord,
My life expires if thou depart;
Be thou, my heart, still near my God,
And thou, my God, be near my heart.

2 I was not born for earth and sin,
Nor can I live on things so vile;
Yet I would stay my Father's time,
And hope and wait for heaven a
while.

3 Then, dearest Lord, in thine embrace
Let me resign my fleeting breath,
And with a smile upon my face
Pass the important hour of death.

Hymn 2:118.

The priesthood of Christ.

1 Blood has a voice to pierce the skies
Revenge, the blood of Abel cries;
But the dear stream when Christ was
slain
Speaks *Peace* as loud from ev'ry vein.

2 Pardon and peace from God on high,
Behold he lays his vengeance by,

And rebels that deserv'd his
 sword,
Become the favourites of the Lord.

3 To Jesus let our praises rise,
Who gave his life a sacrifice;
Now he appears before his God,
And for our pardon pleads his
 blood.

Hymn 2:119.

The holy scriptures.

1 Laden with guilt, and full of fears,
I fly to thee, my Lord,
And not a glimpse of hope appears,
But in thy written word.

2 The volume of my Father's grace
Does all my griefs assuage:
Here I behold my Saviour's face
Almost in every page.

3 [This is the field where hidden lies
The pearl of price unknown,
That merchant is divinely wise
Who makes the pearl his own.]

4 [Here consecrated water flows
To quench my thirst of sin;
Here the fair tree of knowledge grows,
Nor danger dwells therein.]

5 This is the Judge that ends the strife,
Where wit and reason fail;
My guide to everlasting life,
Thro' all this gloomy vale.

6 O may thy counsels, mighty God,
My roving feet command;
Nor I forsake the happy road
That leads to thy right-hand.

Hymn 2:120.

The law and gospel joined in scripture.

1 The Lord declares his will,
And keeps the world in awe;
Amidst the smoke on Sinai's hill
Breaks out his fiery law.

2 The Lord reveals his face,
And smiling from above,
Sends down the gospel of his grace,
Th' epistles of his love.

3 These sacred words impart
Our Maker's just commands;
The pity of his melting heart,
And vengeance of his hands.

4 [Hence we awake our fear,
We draw our comfort hence;
The arms of grace are treasur'd here,
And armour of defence.

5 We learn Christ crucify'd,
And here behold his blood:
All arts and knowledges beside
Will do us little good.]

6 We read the heavenly word,
We take the offer'd grace,
Obey the statutes of the Lord,
And trust his promises.

7 In vain shall Satan rage
Against a book divine;
Where wrath and lightning guard the page,
Where beams of mercy shine.

Hymn 2:121.

The law and gospel distinguished.

1 The law commands, and makes us know
What duties to our God we owe;
But 'Tis the gospel must reveal
Where lies our strength to do his will.

2 The law discovers guilt and sin,
And shews how vile our hearts have
been;
Only the gospel can express
Forgiving love and cleansing grace.

3 What curses doth the law denounce
Against the man that fails but once!
But in the gospel Christ appears
Pardoning the guilt of numerous years.

4 My soul, no more attempt to draw
Thy life and comfort from the law,
Fly to the hope the gospel gives;
The man that trusts the promise
lives.

Hymn 2:122.

Retirement and meditation.

1 My God, permit me not to be
A stranger to myself and thee;

Amidst a thousand thoughts I rove
Forgetful of my highest love.

2 Why should my passions mix with earth,
And thus debase my heavenly birth?
Why should I cleave to things below,
And let my God, my Saviour go?

3 Call me away from flesh and sense,
One sovereign word can draw me thence;
I would obey the voice divine,
And all inferior joys resign.

4 Be earth with all her scenes withdrawn,
Let noise and vanity be gone;
In secret silence of the mind,
My heaven, and there my God I find.

Hymn 2:123.

The benefit of public ordinances.

1 Away from every mortal care,
Away from earth our souls retreat;
We leave this worthless world afar,
And wait and worship near thy seat.

2 Lord, in the temple of thy grace
We see thy feet, and we adore;
We gaze upon thy lovely face,
And learn the wonders of thy
power.

3 While here our various wants we
mourn,
United groans ascend on high,
And prayer bears a quick return
Of blessings in variety.

4 [If Satan rage and sin grow strong,
Here we receive some cheering
word;
We gird the gospel armour on
To fight the battles of the Lord.

5 Or if our spirit faints and dies,
(Our conscience gall'd with inward
stings)
Here doth the righteous sun arise
With healing beams beneath his
wings.]

6 Father, my soul would still abide
Within thy temple, near thy side;
But if my feet must hence depart
Still keep thy dwelling in my heart.

Hymn 2:124.

Moses, Aaron, and Joshua.

1 'Tis not the law of ten commands
On holy Sinai given,
Or sent to men by Moses' hands,
Can bring us safe to heaven.

2 'Tis not the blood which Aaron spilt,
Nor smoke of sweetest smell,
Can buy a pardon for our guilt,
Or save our souls from hell.

3 Aaron the priest resigns his breath
At God's immediate will;
And in the desert yields to death
Upon th' appointed hill.

4 And thus on Jordan's yonder side
The tribes of Israel stand,
While Moses bow'd his head and dy'd
Short of the promis'd land.

5 Israel rejoice, now Joshua * leads,
He'll bring your tribes to rest;

---

* Joshua, the same with Jesus, and signifies a Saviour.

So far the Saviour's name exceeds
The ruler and the priest.

Hymn 2:125.

Faith and repentance; unbelief and impenitence.

1 Life and immortal joys are given
To those that mourn the sins they've done,
Children of wrath made heirs of heaven
By faith in God's eternal Son.

2 Woe to the wretch that never felt
The inward pangs of pious grief,
But adds to all his crying guilt
The stubborn sin of unbelief.

3 The law condemns the rebel dead,
Under the wrath of God he lies,
He seals the curse on his own head,
And with a double vengeance dies.

Hymn 2:126.

God glorified in the gospel.

1 The Lord, descending from above,
Invites his children near,
While power and truth and
boundless love
Display their glories here.

2 Here in thy gospel's wondrous
frame
Fresh wisdom we pursue;
A thousand angels learn thy
Name
Beyond whate'er they knew.

3 Thy Name is writ in fairest lines,
Thy wonders here we trace;
Wisdom thro' all the mystery
shines,
And shines in Jesu's face.

4 The law its best obedience owes
To our incarnate God;
And thy revenging justice shows
Its honours in his blood.

6 But still the lustre of thy grace
Our warmer thoughts employs,
Gilds the whole scene with brighter
rays,
And more exalts our joys.

Hymn 2:127.

Circumcision and baptism. (Written only for those who practise infant baptism.)

1 Thus did the sons of Abrah'm pass
Under the bloody seal of grace;
The young disciples bore the yoke,
Till Christ the painful bondage broke.

2 By milder ways doth Jesus prove
His Father's covenant, and his love;
He seals to saints his glorious grace,
And not forbids their infant race.

3 Their seed is sprinkled with his blood,
Their children set apart for God,
His Spirit on their offspring shed,
Like water pour'd upon the head.

4 Let every saint with cheerful voice
In this large covenant rejoice;
Young children in their early days
Shall give the God of Abrah'm praise.

Hymn 2:128.

Corrupt nature from Adam.

1 Bless'd with the joy of innocence
Adam, our father, stood,
Till he debas'd his soul to sense,
And ate th' unlawful food.

2 Now we are born a sensual race,
To sinful joys inclin'd;
Reason has lost its native place,
And flesh enslaves the mind.

3 While flesh and sense and passion
reigns,
Sin is the sweetest good:
We fancy music in our chains,
And so forget the load.

4 Great God, renew our ruin'd frame,
Our broken powers restore,
Inspire us with a heavenly flame,
And flesh shall reign no more.

5 Eternal Spirit, write thy law
Upon our inward parts,

And let the second Adam draw
His image on our hearts.

Hymn 2:129.

We walk by faith, not by sight.

1 'Tis by the faith of joys to come
We walk thro' deserts dark as night;
Till we arrive at heaven our home,
Faith is our guide, and faith our
light.

2 The want of sight she well supplies,
She makes the pearly gates appear;
Far into distant worlds she pries,
And brings eternal glories near.

3 Cheerful we tread the desert thro',
While faith inspires a heavenly ray,
Tho' lions roar, and tempests blow,
And rocks and dangers fill the way.

4 So Abrah'm, by divine command,
Left his own house to walk with God;
His faith beheld the promis'd land,
And fir'd his zeal along the road.

Hymn 2:130.

The new creation.

1 Attend while God's exalted Son
Doth his own glories shew;
"Behold I sit upon my throne
Creating all things new.

2 "Nature and sin are pass'd away,
And the old Adam dies;
"My hands a new foundation lay,
"See the new world arise.

3 "I'll be a sun of righteousness
"To the new-heavens I make;
"None but the new-born heirs of grace
"My glories shall partake."

4 Mighty Redeemer, set me free
From my old state of sin;
O make my soul alive to thee,
Create new powers within.

5 Renew mine eyes, and form mine ears,
And mould my heart afresh;

Give me new passions, joys and fears,
And turn the stone to flesh.

6 Far from the regions of the dead,
From sin, and earth, and hell,
In the new-world that grace has made
I would for ever dwell.

Hymn 2:131.

The excellency of the Christian religion.

1 Let everlasting glories crown
Thy head, my Saviour and my Lord;
Thy hands have brought salvation down,
And writ the blessings in thy word.

2 [What if we trace the globe around,
And search from Britain to Japan,
There shall be no religion found
So just to God, so safe for man.]

3 In vain the trembling conscience seeks
Some solid ground to rest upon;
With long despair the spirit breaks,
Till we apply to Christ alone.

4 How well thy blessed truths agree!
How wise and holy thy commands!
Thy promises how firm they be!
How firm our hope and comfort
stands!

5 [Not the feign'd fields of heathenish
bliss
Could raise such pleasures in the
mind;
Nor does the Turkish paradise
Pretend to joys so well refin'd.]

6 Should all the forms that men
devise
Assault my faith with treacherous
art,
I'd call them vanity and lies
And bind the gospel to my heart.

Hymn 2:132.

The offices of Christ.

1 We bless the Prophet of the Lord,
That comes with truth and grace;
Jesus, thy Spirit and thy word
Shall lead us in thy ways.

2 We reverence our High Priest above,
Who offer'd up his blood,
And lives to carry on his love,
By pleading with our God.

3 We honour our exalted King,
How sweet are his commands!
He guards our souls from hell and sin
By his almighty hands.

4 Hosanna to his glorious Name,
Who saves by different ways;
His mercies lay a sovereign claim
To our immortal praise.

Hymn 2:133.

The operations of the Holy Spirit.

1 Eternal Spirit! we confess
And sing the wonders of thy grace;
Thy power conveys our blessings down
From God the Father and the Son.

2 Enlighten'd by thine heavenly ray
Our shades and darkness turn to day;
Thine inward teachings make us know
Our danger and our refuge too.

3 Thy power and glory works within,
And breaks the chains of reigning sin,
Doth our imperious lusts subdue,
And forms our wretched hearts
anew.

4 The troubled conscience knows thy
voice,
Thy cheering words awake our joys;
Thy words allay the stormy wind,
And calm the surges of the mind.

Hymn 2:134.

Circumcision abolished.

1 The promise was divinely free,
Extensive was the grace;
"I will the God of Abrah'm be,
"And of his numerous race."

2 He said; and with a bloody seal
Confirm'd the words he spoke;
Long did the Sons of Abrah'm feel
The sharp and painful yoke.

3 Till God's own Son, descending low,
Gave his own flesh to bleed;

And Gentiles taste the blessing now,
From the hard bondage freed.

4 The God of Abrah'm claims our praise,
His promises endure;
And Christ the Lord in gentler ways
Makes the salvation sure.

Hymn 2:135.

Types and prophecies of Christ.

1 Behold the woman's promis'd seed!
Behold the great Messiah come!
Behold the prophets all agreed
To give him the superior room!

2 Abrah'm the saint rejoic'd of old
When visions of the Lord he saw;
Moses the man of God foretold
This great fulfiller of his law.

3 The types bore witness to his Name,
Obtain'd their chief design, and ceas'd;
The incense and the bleeding lamb,
The ark, the altar, and the priest.

4 Predictions in abundance meet
To join their blessings on his head;
Jesus, we worship at thy feet,
And nations own the promis'd seed.

Hymn 2:136.

Miracles at the birth of Christ.

1 The King of Glory sends his Son
To make his entrance on this earth!
Behold the midnight bright as noon,
And heavenly hosts declare his
birth!

2 About the young Redeemer's head
What wonders and what glories
meet!
An unknown star arose, and led
The eastern sages to his feet.

3 Simeon and Anna both conspire
The Infant-Saviour to proclaim;
Inward they felt the sacred fire,
And bless'd the babe, and own'd his
Name.

4 Let Jews and Greeks blaspheme aloud,
And treat the holy Child with scorn;
Our souls adore th' eternal God
Who condescended to be born.

Hymn 2:137.

Miracles in the life, death, and resurrection of Christ.

1 Behold the blind their sight receive;
Behold the dead awake and live;
The dumb speak wonders, and the lame
Leap like the hart, and bless his Name.

2 Thus doth th' eternal Spirit own
And seal the mission of the Son;
The Father vindicates his cause,
While he hangs bleeding on the cross.

3 He dies; the heavens in mourning stood;
He rises, and appears a God;
Behold the Lord ascending high,
No more to bleed, no more to die.

4 Hence and for ever from my heart
I bid my doubts and fears depart;
And to those hands my soul resign
Which bear credentials so divine.

Hymn 2:138.

The power of the gospel.

1 This is the word of truth and love,
Sent to the nations from above;
Jehovah here resolves to shew
What his almighty grace can do.

2 This remedy did wisdom find
To heal diseases of the mind:
This sovereign balm, whose virtues can
Restore the ruin'd creature, man.

3 The gospel bids the dead revive,
Sinners obey the voice, and live;
Dry bones are rais'd and cloth'd afresh,
And hearts of stone are turn'd to
flesh.

4 [Where Satan reign'd in shades of
night
The gospel strikes a heavenly light;

Our lusts its wondrous power
controls,
And calms the rage of angry souls.]

5 [Lions and beasts of savage name
Put on the nature of the lamb;
Whilst the wild world esteems it
strange
Gaze, and admire, and hate the
change.]

6 May but this grace my soul renew,
Let sinners gaze and hate me too;
The word that saves me does engage
A sure defence from all their rage.

Hymn 2:139.

The example of Christ.

1 My dear Redeemer and my Lord,
I read my duty in thy word;
But in thy life the law appears
Drawn out in living characters.

2 Such was thy truth, and such thy zeal,
Such deference to thy Father's will,
Such love, and meekness so divine,

I would transcribe, and make them
mine.

3 Cold mountains and the midnight air
Witness'd the fervor of thy prayer:
The desert thy temptations knew,
Thy conflict and thy victory too.

4 Be thou my pattern; make me bear
More of thy gracious image here;
Then God the Judge shall own my
name,
Amongst the followers of the Lamb.

Hymn 2:140.

The example: of Christ and the saints.

1 Give me the wings of faith to rise
Within the veil, and see
The saints above, how great their joys,
How bright their glories be.

2 Once they were mourning here
below,
And wet their couch with tears;
They wrestled hard, as we do now,
With sins, and doubts, and fears.

3 I ask them whence their victory came,
They, with united breath,
Ascribe their conquest to the Lamb,
Their triumph to his death.

4 They mark'd the footsteps that he
trod,
(His zeal inspir'd their breast;)
And following their incarnate God
Possess the promis'd rest.

5 Our glorious Leader claims our
praise
For his own pattern given,
While the long cloud of witnesses
Shew the same path to heaven.

Hymn 2:141.

Faith assisted by sense; or, Preaching, baptism, and the Lord's Supper.

1 My Saviour-God, my Sovereign-
Prince
Reigns far above the skies;
But brings his graces down to
sense,
And helps my faith to rise.

2 My eyes and ears shall bless his
Name,
They read and hear his word;
My touch and taste shall do the
same
When they receive the Lord.

3 Baptismal water is design'd
To seal his cleansing grace;
While at his feast of bread and
wine
He gives his saints a place.

4 But not the waters of a flood
Can make my flesh so clean,
As by his Spirit and his blood
He'll wash my soul from sin.

5 Not choicest meats or noblest
wines,
So much my heart refresh,
As when my faith goes thro' the
signs,
And feeds upon his flesh.

6 I love the Lord, that stoops so low
To give his word a seal;
But the rich grace his hands bestow
Exceeds the figures still.

Hymn 2:142.

Faith in Christ our sacrifice.

1 Not all the blood of beasts
On Jewish altars slain
Could give the guilty conscience
peace,
Or wash away the stain.

2 But Christ the heavenly Lamb
Takes all our sins away;
A sacrifice of nobler name
And richer blood than they.

3 My faith would lay her hand
On that dear head of thine,
While like a penitent I stand
And there confess my sin.

4 My soul looks back to see
The burdens thou didst bear
When hanging on the cursed tree,
And hopes her guilt was there.

5 Believing we rejoice
To see the curse remove;
We bless the Lamb with cheerful voice,
And sing his bleeding love.

Hymn 2:143.

Flesh and spirit.

1 What different powers of grace and sin
Attend our mortal state!
I hate the thoughts that work within,
And do the works I hate.

2 Now I complain, and groan, and die,
While sin and Satan reign:
Now raise my songs of triumph high,
For grace prevails again.

3 So darkness struggles with the light
Till perfect day arise;
Water and fire maintain the fight
Until the weaker dies.

4 Thus will the flesh and spirit strive,
And vex and break my peace;
But I shall quit this mortal life,
And sin for ever cease.

Hymn 2:144.

The effusion of the Spirit; or, The success of the gospel.

1 Great was the day, the joy was great,
When the divine disciples met;
Whilst on their heads the Spirit came,
And sat like tongues of cloven
flame.

2 What gifts, what miracles he gave!
And power to kill, and power to save!
Furnish'd their tongues with
wondrous words,
Instead of shields, and spears, and
swords.

3 Thus arm'd, he sent the champions
forth
From east to west, from south to north;
"Go, and assert your Saviour's cause,
"Go, spread the mystery of his
cross."

4 These weapons of the holy war,
Of what almighty force they are
To make our stubborn passions bow,
And lay the proudest rebel low!

5 Nations, the learned and the rude,
Are by these heavenly arms subdu'd;
While Satan rages at his loss,
And hates the doctrine of the cross.

6 Great King of Grace, my heart subdue,
I would be led in triumph too,
A willing captive to my Lord,
And sing the victories of his word.

Hymn 2:145.

Sight through a glass, and face to face.

1 I love the windows of thy grace
Thro' which my Lord is seen,
And long to meet my Saviour's face
Without a glass between.

2 O, that the happy hour were come
To change my faith to sight!
I shall behold my Lord at home
In a diviner light.

3 Haste, my beloved, and remove
These interposing days:
Then shall my passions all be love,
And all my powers be praise.

Hymn 2:146.

The vanity of creatures; or, No rest on earth.

1 Man has a soul of vast desires,
He burns within with restless fires;
Tost to and fro, his passions fly
From vanity to vanity.

2 In vain on earth we hope to find
Some solid good to fill the mind,
We try new pleasures, but we feel
The inward thirst and torment still.

3 So when a raging fever burns
We shift from side to side by turns,
And 'Tis a poor relief we gain
To change the place, but keep the pain.

4 Great God, subdue this vicious thirst,
This love to vanity and dust;
Cure the vile fever of the mind,
And feed our souls with joys refin'd.

Hymn 2:147.

The creation of the world, Gen. 1.

1 "Now let a spacious world arise,"
Said the Creator-Lord:
At once the obedient earth and skies
Rose at his sovereign word.

2 [Dark was the deep; the waters lay
Confus'd and drown'd the land:
He call'd the light; the new-born day
Attends on his command.

3 He bids the clouds ascend on high;
The clouds ascend and bear
A watery treasure to the sky,
And float on softer air.

4 The liquid element below
Was gather'd by his hand;
The rolling seas together flow,
And leave the solid land.

5 With herbs and plants, a flowery birth,
The naked globe he crown'd,
Ere there was rain to bless the earth,
Or sun to warm the ground.

6 Then he adorn'd the upper skies;
Behold the sun appears,
The moon and stars in order rise
To make our months and years,

7 Out of the deep th' almighty King
Did vital beings frame;
The painted fowls of every wing,
And fish of every name.]

8 He gave the lion and the worm
At once their wondrous birth;
And grazing beasts of various form,
Rose from the teeming earth.

9 Adam was fram'd of equal clay,
Tho' sovereign of the rest,
Design'd for nobler ends than they,
With God's own image bless'd.

10 Thus glorious in the Maker's eye
The young creation stood;
He saw the building from on high,
His word pronounc'd it good.

11 Lord, while the frame of nature stands,
Thy praise shall fill my tongue;
But the new world of grace demands
A more exalted song.

Hymn 2:148.

God reconciled in Christ.

1 Dearest of all the names above
My Jesus, and my God,
Who can resist thy heavenly love,
Or trifle with thy blood?

2 'Tis by the merits of thy death
The Father smiles again;
'Tis by thine interceding breath
The Spirit dwells with men.

3 Till God in human flesh I see,
My thoughts no comfort find;
The holy, just, and sacred Three
Are terrors to my mind.

4 But if Immanuel's face appear,
My hope, my joy, begins;
His Name forbids my slavish fear,
His grace removes my sins.

5 While Jews on their own law rely,
And Greeks of wisdom boast,
I love th' incarnate mystery,
And there I fix my trust.

Hymn 2:149.

Honour to Magistrates; or, Government from God.

1 Eternal Sovereign of the sky,
And Lord of all below,
We mortals to thy majesty
Our first obedience owe.

2 Our souls adore thy throne supreme,
And bless thy providence
For magistrates of meaner name,
Our glory and defence.

3 [The crowns of British princes shine
With rays above the rest,
Where laws and liberties combine
To make the nation bless'd.]

4 Kingdoms on firm foundations stand,
While virtue finds reward;
And sinners perish from the land
By justice and the sword.

5 Let Cesar's due be ever paid
To Cesar and his throne;
But consciences and souls were made
To be the Lord's alone.

Hymn 2:150.

The deceitfulness of sin.

1 Sin has a thousand treacherous
arts
To practise on the mind;
With flattering looks she tempts our

hearts
But leaves a sting behind.

2 With names of virtue she deceives
The aged and the young;
And while the heedless wretch believes,
She makes his fetters strong.

3 She pleads for all the joys she brings,
And gives a fair pretence;
But cheats the soul of heavenly things,
And chains it down to sense.

4 So on a tree divinely fair
Grew the forbidden food;
Our mother took the poison there,
And tainted all her blood.

Hymn 2:151.

Prophesy and inspiration.

1 'Twas by an order from the Lord
The ancient prophets spoke his word;
His Spirit did their tongues inspire,

And warm'd their hearts with heavenly fire.

2 The works and wonders which they wrought
Confirm'd the messages they brought;
The prophet's pen succeeds his breath
To save the holy words from death.

3 Great God, mine eyes with pleasure look
On the dear volume of thy book;
There my Redeemer's face I see,
And read his name who dy'd for me.

4 Let the false raptures of the mind
Be lost and vanish in the wind;
Here I can fix my hopes secure,
This is thy word, and must endure.

Hymn 2:152.

Sinai and Sion, Heb. 12. 18 &c.

1 Not to the terrors of the Lord,
The tempest, fire, and smoke,

Not to the thunder of that word
Which God on Sinai spoke;

2 But we are come to Sion's hill,
The city of our God,
Where milder words declare his will
And spread his love abroad.

3 Behold th' innumerable host
Of angels cloth'd in light!
Behold the spirits of the just
Whose faith is turn'd to sight!

4 Behold the bless'd assembly there,
Whose names are writ in heaven;
And God the judge of all declares
Their vilest sins forgiven.

5 The saints on earth and all the
dead
But one communion make;
All join in Christ their living head,
And of his grace partake.

6 In such society as this
My weary soul would rest:
The man that dwells where Jesus is,
Must be for ever blest.

Hymn 2:153.

The distemper, folly, and madness of sin.

1 Sin like a venomous disease
Infects our vital blood;
The only balm is sovereign grace,
And the physician, God.

2 Our beauty and our strength are fled,
And we draw near to death;
But Christ the Lord recalls the dead
With his almighty breath.

3 Madness by nature reigns within,
The passions burn and rage;
Till God's own Son with skill divine
The inward fire assuage.

4 [We lick the dust, we grasp the wind,
And solid good despise;
Such is the folly of the mind,
Till Jesus makes us wise.

5 We give our souls the wounds they feel,
We drink the poisonous gall,
And rush with fury down to hell;
But heaven prevents the fall.]

6 [The man possess'd amongst the tombs,
Cuts his own flesh and cries;
He foams, and raves, till Jesus comes,
And the foul spirit flies.]

Hymn 2:154.

Self-righteousness insufficient.

1 "Where are the mourners, [1] (saith the Lord)
"That wait and tremble at my word,
"That walk in darkness all the day?
"Come, make my name your trust and stay.

2 ["No works nor duties of your own
"Can for the smallest sin atone;
"The robes[2] that nature may provide
"Will not your least pollutions hide.

3 "The softest couch that nature knows
"Can give the conscience no repose:

[1] Isaiah 1:10-11.
[2] Isaiah 28:20.

"Look to my righteousness, and live;
"Comfort and peace are mine to give.]

4 "Ye sons of pride that kindle coals
"With your own hands to warm your souls,
"Walk in the light of your own fire,
"Enjoy the sparks that ye desire.

5 "This is your portion at my hands;
"Hell waits you with her iron bands,
"Ye shall lie down in sorrow there,
"In death, in darkness, and despair."

Hymn 2:155.

Christ our passover.

1 Lo the destroying angel flies
To Pharaoh's stubborn land:
The pride and flower of Egypt dies
By his vindictive hand.

2 He pass'd the tents of Jacob o'er,
Nor pour'd the wrath divine;
He saw the blood on every door,
And bless'd the peaceful sign.

3 Thus th' appointed Lamb must
bleed
To break th' Egyptian yoke;
Thus Israel is from bondage freed,
And 'scapes the angel's stroke.

4 Lord, if my heart were sprinkled too
With blood so rich as thine,
Justice no longer would pursue
This guilty soul of mine.

5 Jesus our passover was slain,
And has at once procur'd
Freedom from Satan's heavy chain,
And God's avenging sword.

Hymn 2:156.

Presumption and despair; or, Satan's various temptations.

1 I hate the tempter and his charms,
I hate his flattering breath;
The serpent takes a thousand forms
To cheat our souls to death.

2 He feeds our hopes with airy dreams,
Or kills with slavish fear;

And holds us still in wide extremes,
Presumption, or despair.

3 Now he persuades, “How easy ’Tis
“To walk the road to heaven;”
Anon he swells our sins, and cries,
“They cannot be forgiven.”

4 [He bids young sinners, “Yet forbear
“To think of God or death;
“For prayer and devotion are
“But melancholy breath.”

5 He tells the aged, “They must die,
“And ’Tis too late to pray;
“In vain for mercy now they cry,
“For they have lost their day.”]

6 Thus he supports his cruel throne
By mischief and deceit;
And drags the sons of Adam down
To darkness and the pit.

7 Almighty God, cut short his power,
Let him in darkness dwell;
And, that he vex the earth no more,
Confine him down to hell.

Hymn 2:157.

The same.

1 Now Satan comes with dreadful roar,
And threatens to destroy;
He worries whom he can't devour
With a malicious joy.

2 Ye sons of God, oppose his rage,
Resist, and he'll be gone;
Thus did our dearest Lord engage
And vanquish him alone.

3 Now he appears almost divine
Like innocence and love,
But the old serpent lurks within
When he assumes the dove.

4 Fly from the false deceiver's tongue,
Ye Sons of Adam, fly;
Our parents found the snare too strong,
Nor should the children try.

Hymn 2:158.

Few saved; or, The almost Christian,
the hypocrite, and apostate.

1 Broad is the road that leads to death,
And thousands walk together there;
But wisdom shews a narrower path,
With here and there a traveller.

2 "Deny thyself, and take thy cross,"
Is the Redeemer's great command;
Nature must count her gold but dross
If she would gain this heavenly land.

3 The fearful soul that tires and faints,
And walks the ways of God no more,
Is but esteem'd almost a saint,
And makes his own destruction sure.

4 Lord, let not all my hopes be vain;
Create my heart entirely new,
Which hypocrites could ne'er attain,
Which false apostates never knew.

Hymn 2:159.

An unconverted state; or, Converting grace.

1 [Great King of Glory and of grace,
We own with humble shame,

How vile is our degenerate race,
And our first father's name.]

2 From Adam flows our tainted blood,
The poison reigns within,
Makes us averse to all that's good,
And willing slaves to sin.

3 [Daily we break thy holy laws,
And then reject thy grace;
Engag'd in the old serpent's cause
Against our Maker's face.]

4 We live estrang'd afar from God,
And love the distance well;
With haste we run the dangerous road
That leads to death and hell.

5 And can such rebels be restor'd?
Such natures made divine?
Let sinners see thy glory, Lord,
And feel this power of thine.

6 We raise our Father's name on high,
Who his own Spirit sends
To bring rebellious strangers nigh,
And turn his foes to friends.

Hymn 2:160.

Custom in sin.

1 Let the wild leopards of the wood
Put off the spots that nature gives,
Then may the wicked turn to God,
And change their tempers and their lives.

2 As well might Ethiopian slaves
Wash out the darkness of their skin;
The dead as well might leave their graves,
As old transgressors cease to sin.

3 Where vice has held its empire long
'Twill not endure the least control;
None but a power divinely strong
Can turn the current of the soul.

4 Great God, I own thy power divine,
That works to change this heart of mine;
I would be form'd anew, and bless
The wonders of creating grace.

Hymn 2:161.

Christian virtues; or, The difficulty of conversion.

1 Strait is the way, the door is strait
That leads to joys on high;
'Tis but a few that find the gate,
While crowds mistake and die.

2 Beloved self must be deny'd,
The mind and will renew'd:
Passion suppress'd, and patience try'd,
And vain desires subdu'd.

3 [Flesh is a dangerous foe to grace,
Where it prevails and rules;
Flesh must be humbled, pride abas'd,
Lest they destroy our souls.

4 The love of gold be banish'd hence,
(That vile idolatry);
And every member, every sense
In sweet subjection lie.]

5 The tongue, that most unruly power,
Requires a strong restraint;

We must be watchful every hour,
And pray, but never faint.

6 Lord, can a feeble helpless worm
Fulfil a task so hard?
Thy grace must all my work perform,
And give the free reward.

Hymn 2:162

Meditation of heaven; or, The joy of faith.

1 My thoughts surmount these lower
  skies
And look within the veil;
There springs of endless pleasure rise,
The waters never fail.

2 There I behold with sweet delight
The blessed Three in One;
And strong affections fix my sight
On God's incarnate Son.

3 His promise stands for ever firm,
His grace shall ne'er depart;
He binds my name upon his arm,
And seals it on his heart.

4 Light are the pains that' nature brings,
How short our sorrows are,
When with eternal future things,
The present we compare!

5 I would not be a stranger still
To that celestial place,
Where I for ever hope to dwell
Near my Redeemer's face.

Hymn 2:163.

Complaint of desertion and temptations.

1 Dear Lord, behold our sore distress;
Our sins attempt to reign;
Stretch out thine arm of conquering
  grace,
And let thy foes be slain.

2 [The lion with his dreadful roar
Affrights thy feeble sheep;
Reveal the glory of thy power,
And chain him to the deep.

3 Must we indulge a long despair,
Shall our petitions die;

Our mournings never reach thine ear,
Nor tears affect thine eye?]

4 If thou despise a mortal groan,
Yet hear a Saviour's blood;
An Advocate so near the throne
Pleads and prevails with God.

5 He bought the Spirit's powerful sword
To slay our deadly foes;
Our sins shall die beneath thy word,
And hell in vain oppose.

6 How boundless is our Father's grace,
In height and depth, and length!
He makes his Son our righteousness,
His Spirit is our strength.

Hymn 2:164.

The end of the world.

1 Why should this earth delight us so?
Why should we fix our eyes
On these low grounds where sorrows grow,
And every pleasure dies?

2 While time his sharpest teeth
prepares
Our comforts to devour,
There is a land above the stars,
And joys above his power.

3 Nature shall be dissolv'd and die,
The sun must end his race,
The earth and sea for ever fly
Before my Saviour's face.

4 When will that glorious morning
rise!
When the last trumpet sound,
And call the nations to the skies
From underneath the ground?

Hymn 2:165.

Unfruitfulness, ignorance, and unsanctified affections.

1 Long have I sat beneath the sound
Of thy salvation, Lord
But still how weak my faith is
found,
And knowledge of thy word!

2 Oft I frequent thy holy place
And hear almost in vain;
How small a portion of thy grace
My memory can retain!

3 [My dear Almighty, and my God,
How little art thou known
By all the judgments of thy rod,
And blessings of thy throne!]

4 [How cold and feeble is my love!
How negligent my fear!
How low my hope of joys above!
How few affections there!]

5 Great God, thy sovereign power impart
To give thy word success:
Write the salvation in my heart,
And make me learn the grace.

6 [Shew my forgetful feet the way
That leads to joys on high;
There knowledge grows without
decay,
And love shall never die.]

Hymn 2:166.

The divine perfections.

1 How shall I praise th' eternal God,
That infinite unknown?
Who can ascend his high abode,
Or venture near his throne?

2 [The great Invisible! he dwells
Conceal'd in dazzling light;
But his all-searching eye reveals
The secrets of the night.

3 Those watchful eyes that never sleep
Survey the world around;
His wisdom is a boundless deep
Where all our thoughts are
drown'd.]

4 [Speak we of strength? His arm is
strong
To save or to destroy:
Infinite years his life prolong,
And endless is his joy.]

5 [He knows no shadow of a change,
Nor alters his decrees;
Firm as a rock his truth remains
To guard his promises.]

6 [Sinners before his presence die;
How holy is his Name!

His anger and his jealousy
Burn like devouring flame.]

7 Justice upon a dreadful throne
Maintains the rights of God;
While Mercy sends her pardons down,
Bought with a Saviour's blood.

8 Now to my soul, immortal King,
Speak some forgiving word;
Then 't will be double joy to sing
The glories of my Lord.

Hymn 2:167.

The divine perfections.

1 Great God, thy glories shall employ
My holy fear, my humble joy;
My lips in songs of honour bring
Their tribute to th' eternal King.

2 [Earth and the stars and worlds unknown,
Depend precarious on his throne,
All nature hangs upon his word,
And grace and glory own their Lord.]

3 [His sovereign power what mortal knows?
If he command who dares oppose?
With strength he girds himself around,
And treads the rebels to the ground.]

4 [Who shall pretend to teach him skill?
Or guide the counsels of his will?
His wisdom like a sea divine,
Flows deep and high beyond our line.]

5 [His Name is holy, and his eye
Burns with immortal jealousy;
He hates the sons of pride, and sheds
His fiery vengeance on their heads.]

6 [The beamings of his piercing sight
Bring dark hypocrisy to light;
Death and destruction naked lie,
And hell uncover'd to his eye.]

7 [Th' eternal law before him stands;
His justice with impartial hands

Divides to all their due reward,
Or by the sceptre or the sword.]

8 [His mercy like a boundless sea
Washes our loads of guilt away,
While his own Son came down and
dy'd,
T' engage his justice on our side.]

9 [Each of his words demands my faith,
My soul can rest on all he saith;
His truth inviolably keeps
The largest promise of his lips.]

10 O tell me with a gentle voice,
"Thou art my God," and I'll rejoice!
Fill'd with thy love, I dare proclaim
The brightest honours of thy Name.

Hymn 2:168.

The same.

1 Jehovah reigns, his throne is high,
His robes are light and majesty;
His glory shines with beams so bright
No mortal can sustain the sight.

2 His terrors keep the world in awe,
His justice guards his holy law;
His love reveals a smiling face,
His truth and promise seal the grace.

3 Thro' all his works his wisdom
shines,
And baffles Satan's deep designs;
His power is sovereign to fulfil
The noblest counsels of his will.

4 And will this glorious
Lord descend
To be my father and my friend?
Then let my songs with
angels join;
Heaven is secure if God be mine.

Hymn 2:169.

As the 148th Psalm. The same.

1 The Lord Jehovah reigns
His throne is built on high;
The garments he assumes
Are light and majesty;
His glories shine
With beams so bright

No mortal eye
Can bear the sight.

2 The thunders of his hand
Keep the wide world in awe;
His wrath and justice stand
To guard his holy law;
And where his love
Resolves to bless,
His truth confirms
And seals the grace.

3 Thro' all his ancient works
Surprising wisdom shines,
Confounds the powers of hell,
And breaks their curs'd designs:
Strong is his arm,
And shall fulfil
His great decrees,
His sovereign will.

4 And can this mighty King
Of Glory condescend?
And will he write his Name,
"My Father and my Friend?"
I love his Name,
I love his word;
Join all my powers,
And praise the Lord.

Hymn 2:170.

God incomprehensible and sovereign.

1 Can creatures to perfection find[1]
Th' eternal uncreated mind?
Or can the largest stretch of thought
Measure and search his nature out?

2 'Tis high as heaven, 'tis deep as hell,
And what can mortals know or tell?
His glory spreads beyond the sky,
And all the shining worlds on high.

3 But man, vain man, would fain be wise,
Born like a wild young colt he flies
Thro' all the follies of his mind,
And swells and snuffs the empty wind.

4 God is a King of power unknown,
Firm are the orders of his throne;
If he resolve, who dares oppose,
Or ask him why, or what he does?

[1] Job 11:7 &c.

5 He wounds the heart, and he makes
whole;
He calms the tempest of the soul;
When he shuts up in long despair
Who can remove the heavy bar?

6 He frowns,[2] and darkness veils the
moon;
The fainting sun grows dim at noon;
The pillars[3] of heaven's starry roof
Tremble and start at his reproof.

7 He gave the vaulted heaven its form,
The crooked serpent and the worm;
He breaks the billows with his
breath,
And smites the Sons of pride to
death.

8 These are a portion of his ways,
But who shall dare describe his
face?
Who can endure his light, or stand
To hear the thunders of his hand?

END OF THE SECOND BOOK.

---

[2] Job 25:5.
[3] Job 26:11 &c.

Hymns

Book 3
Prepared for the Lord's Supper

Hymn 3:1.

The Lord's Supper instituted,
1 Corinthians 11:23 &c.

1 'Twas on that dark, that doleful
night
When powers of earth and hell arose
Against the Son of God's delight,
And friends betray'd him to his foes;

2 Before the mournful scene began
He took the bread, and bless'd, and
brake:
What love thro' all his actions ran!
What wondrous words of grace he
spake!

3 "This is my body broke for sin,
"Receive and eat the living food:"
Then took the cup, and bless'd the
wine;
"'Tis the new covenant in my blood."

4 [For us his flesh with nails was torn,
He bore the scourge, he felt the
thorn;
And justice pour'd upon his head
Its heavy vengeance in our stead.

5 For us his vital blood was spilt,
To buy the pardon of our guilt,
When for black crimes of biggest size
He gave his soul a sacrifice.]

6 "Do this, (he cry'd) till time shall end,
"In memory of your dying Friend;
"Meet at my table, and record
"The love of your departed Lord."

7 [Jesus, thy feast we celebrate,
We shew thy death, we sing thy Name,
Till thou return, and we shall eat
The marriage-supper of the Lamb.]

Hymn 3:2.

Communion with Christ, and with saints, 1 Cor. 10. 16 17.

1 [Jesus invites his saints
To meet around his board;

Here pardon'd rebels sit, and
  hold
Communion with their Lord.

2 For food he gives his flesh,
He bids us drink his blood,
Amazing favour! matchless
  grace
Of our descending God!]

3 This holy bread and wine
Maintains our fainting breath,
By union with our living Lord,
And interest in his death.

4 Our heavenly Father calls
Christ and his members one;
We the young children of his love,
And he the first-born Son.

5 We are but several parts
Of the same broken bread;
One body hath its several limbs,
But Jesus is the head.

6 Let all our powers be join'd
His glorious Name to raise;
Pleasure and love fill every mind,
And every voice be praise.

Hymn 3:3.

The new testament in the blood of Christ; or, The new covenant sealed.

1 “The promise of my Father’s love
“Shall stand for ever good;”
He said, and gave his soul to death,
And seal’d the grace with blood.

2 To this dear covenant of thy word
I set my worthless name;
I seal th’ engagement to my Lord,
And make my humble claim.

3 Thy light, and strength, and pardoning grace,
And glory shall be mine;
My life and soul, my heart and flesh,
And all my powers are thine.

4 I call that legacy my own
Which Jesus did bequeath;
’Twas purchas’d with a dying groan,
And ratify’d in death.

5 Sweet is the memory of his Name,
Who bless’d us in his will,

And to his testament of love
Made his own life the seal.

Hymn 3:4.

Christ's dying love; or, Our pardon bought at a dear price.

1 How condescending and how kind
Was God's eternal Son!
Our misery reach'd his heavenly
mind,
And pity brought him down.

2 [When Justice by our sins provok'd
Drew forth its dreadful sword,
He gave his soul up to the stroke,
Without a murmuring word.]

3 [He sunk beneath our heavy woes
To raise us to his throne;
There's ne'er a gift his hand bestows
But cost his heart a groan.]

4 This was compassion like a God,
That when the Saviour knew
The price of pardon was his blood,
His pity ne'er withdrew.

5 Now tho' he reigns exalted high,
His love is still as great:
Well he remembers Calvary,
Nor lets his saints forget.

6 [Here we behold his bowels roll,
As kind as when he dy'd;
And see the sorrows of his soul
Bleed thro' his wounded side.]

7 [Here we receive repeated seals
Of Jesus' dying love:
Hard is the wretch that never feels
One soft affection move.]

8 Here let our hearts begin to melt,
While we his death record,
And with our joy for pardon'd guilt
Mourn that we pierc'd the Lord.

Hymn 3:5.

Christ the bread of life, John 6. 31 35 39.

1 Let us adore th' eternal Word,
'Tis he our souls hath fed;
Thou art our living stream, O Lord,
And thou th' immortal bread.

2 [The manna came from lower
skies,
But Jesus from above,
Where the fresh springs of pleasure
rise
And rivers flow with love.

3 The Jews the fathers dy'd at last,
Who ate that heavenly bread;
But these provisions which we
taste
Can raise us from the dead.]

4 Bless'd be the Lord that gives his
flesh
To nourish dying men;
And often spreads his table fresh,
Lest we should faint again.

5 Our souls shall draw their heavenly
breath
While Jesus finds supplies;
Nor shall our graces sink to death,
For Jesus never dies.

6 [Daily our mortal flesh decays,
But Christ our life shall come;
His unresisted power shall raise
Our bodies from the tomb.]

Hymn 3:6.

The memorial of our absent Lord,
John 16. 16. Luke 22. 19. John 14. 3.

1 Jesus is gone above the skies,
Where our weak senses reach him not
And carnal objects court our eyes
To thrust our Saviour from our thought.

2 He knows what wandering hearts we have,
Apt to forget his lovely face;
And to refresh our minds he gave
These kind memorials of his grace.

3 The Lord of life this table spread
With his own flesh and dying blood;
We on the rich provision feed,
And taste the wine, and bless the God.

4 Let sinful sweets be all forgot,
And earth grow less in our esteem;
Christ and his love fill every thought,
And faith and hope be fix'd on him.

5 While he is absent from our sight
'Tis to prepare our souls a place,
That we may dwell in heavenly light,
And live for ever near his face.

6 Our eyes look upwards to the hills
Whence our returning Lord shall
come;
We wait thy chariot's awful wheels
To fetch our longing spirits home.]

Hymn 3:7.

Crucifixion to the world by the cross of Christ, Gal. 6. 14.

1 When I survey the wondrous cross
On which the Prince of Glory dy'd,
My richest gain I count but loss,
And pour contempt on all my pride.

2 Forbid it, Lord, that I should boast,
Save in the death of Christ my God;
All the vain things that charm me most,
I sacrifice them to his blood.

3 See from his head, his hands, his feet,
Sorrow and love flow mingled down;

Did e'er such love and sorrow meet?
Or thorns compose so rich a crown?

4 [His dying crimson like a robe
Spreads o'er his body on the tree;
Then am I dead to all the globe,
And all the globe is dead to me.]

5 Were the whole realm of nature
mine,
That were a present far too small;
Love so amazing, so divine,
Demands my soul, my life, my all.

Hymn 3:8.

The tree of life.

1 Come let us join a joyful tune
To our exalted Lord,
Ye saints on high around his throne,
And we around his board.

2 While once upon this lower ground
Weary and faint ye stood,
What dear refreshments here ye
found
From this immortal food!

3 The tree of life that near the
  throne
In heaven's high garden grows,
Laden with grace, bends gently
  down
Its ever-smiling boughs.

4 [Hovering amongst the leaves there
  stands
The sweet celestial Dove,
And Jesus on the branches hangs
The banner of his love.]

5 ['Tis a young heaven of strange
  delight
While in his shade we sit;
His fruit is pleasing to the sight,
And to the taste as sweet.

6 New life it spreads thro' dying
  hearts,
And cheers the drooping mind;
Vigour and joy the juice imparts
Without a sting behind.]

7 Now let the flaming weapon stand
And guard all Eden's trees;
There's ne'er a plant in all that land
That bears such fruits as these.

8 Infinite grace our souls adore,
Whose wondrous hand has made
This living branch of sovereign
  power
To raise and heal the dead.

Hymn 3:9.

The Spirit, the water, and the blood, John 5. 6.

1 [Let all our tongues be one
To praise our God on high,
Who from his bosom sent his Son
To fetch us strangers nigh.

2 Nor let our voices cease
To sing the Saviour's Name;
Jesus th' ambassador of peace,
How cheerfully he came!

3 It cost him cries and tears
To bring us near to God;
Great was our debt, and he appears
To make the payment good.]

4 [My Saviour's pierced side,
Pour'd out a double flood;

By water we are purify'd
And pardon'd by the blood.

5 Infinite was our guilt,
But he our Priest atones;
On the cold ground his life was
  spilt,
And offer'd with his groans.]

6 Look up, my soul, to him
Whose death was thy desert,
And humbly view the living stream
Flow from his breaking heart.

7 There on the cursed tree
In dying pangs he lies,
Fulfils his Father's great decree,
And all our wants supplies.

8 Thus the Redeemer came
By water and by blood;
And when the Spirit speaks the
  same
We feel his witness good.

9 While the eternal Three
Bear their record above,
Here I believe he dy'd for me,
And seal my Saviour's love.

10 [Lord, cleanse my soul from sin,
Nor let thy grace depart;
Great Comforter, abide within,
And witness to my heart.]

Hymn 3:10.

Christ crucified; the wisdom and power of God.

1 Nature with open volume stands
To spread her Maker's praise abroad;
And every labour of his hands
Shews something worthy of a God.

2 But in the grace that rescu'd man
His brightest form of glory shines;
Here on the cross 'Tis fairest drawn
In precious blood and crimson lines.

3 [Here his whole name appears complete;
Nor wit can guess, nor reason prove
Which of the letters best is writ,
The power, the wisdom, or the love.]

4 Here I behold his inmost heart
Where grace and vengeance strangely join,

Piercing his Son with sharpest smart
To make the purchas'd pleasure
mine.

5 O the sweet wonders of that cross
Where God the Saviour lov'd and dy'd!
Her noblest life my spirit draws
From his dear wounds and bleeding
side.

6 I would for ever speak his Name
In sounds to mortal ears unknown,
With angels join to praise the Lamb,
And worship at his Father's throne.

Hymn 3:11.

Pardon brought in our senses.

1 Lord, how divine thy comforts are!
How heavenly is the place
Where Jesus spreads the sacred feast
Of his redeeming grace!

2 There the rich bounties of our God,
And sweetest glories shine;
There Jesus says, that "I am his,
"And my Beloved's mine."

3 “Here,” (says the kind redeeming Lord,
And shews his wounded side)
“See here the spring of all your joys,
“That open’d when I dy’d.”

4 [He smiles and cheers my mournful heart
And tells of all his pain,
“All this,” says he, “I bore for thee;”
And then he smiles again.]

5 What shall we pay our heavenly King
For grace so vast as this?
He brings our pardon to our eyes,
And seals it with a kiss.

6 [Let such amazing loves as these
Be sounded all abroad,
Such favours are beyond degrees,
And worthy of a God.]

7 [To him that wash’d us in his blood
Be everlasting praise,
Salvation, honour, glory, power,
Eternal as his days.]

Hymn 3:12.

The gospel feast, Luke 14. 16 &c.

1 [How rich are thy provisions Lord!
Thy table furnish'd from above,
The fruits of life o'erspread the board,
The cup o'erflows with heavenly
love.

2 Thine ancient family the Jews,
Were first invited to the feast;
We humbly take what they refuse,
And Gentiles thy salvation taste.

3 We are the poor, the blind, the lame,
And help was far, and death was
nigh,
But at the gospel call we came
And every want receiv'd supply.

4 From the highway that leads to hell,
From paths of darkness and despair,
Lord, we are come with thee to
dwell,
Glad to enjoy thy presence here.]

5 [What shall we pay th' eternal Son,
That left the heaven of his abode,

And to this wretched earth came down
To bring us wanderers back to God?

6 It cost him death to save our lives,
To buy our souls it cost his own;
And all the unknown joys he gives,
Were bought with agonies unknown.

7 Our everlasting love is due
To him that ransom'd sinners lost;
And pity'd rebels when he knew
The vast expense his love would cost.]

Hymn 3:13.

Divine love making a feast, and calling in the guests, Luke 14. 17 22 23.

1 How sweet and awful is the place
With Christ within the doors,
While everlasting love displays
The choicest of her stores!

2 Here every bowel of our God
With soft compassion rolls
Here peace and pardon bought with
blood
Is food for dying souls.

3 [While all our hearts and all our songs
Join to admire the feast,
Each of us cry with thankful tongues,
"Lord, why was I a guest?

4 "Why was I made to hear thy voice,
"And enter while there's room?
"When thousands make a wretched choice,
"And rather starve than come."]

5 'Twas the same love that spread the feast,
That sweetly forc'd us in,
Else we had still refus'd to taste,
And perish'd in our sin.

6 [Pity the nations, O our God,
Constrain the earth to come;
Send thy victorious word abroad,
And bring the strangers home.

7 We long to see thy churches full,
That all the chosen race
May with one voice and heart and soul,
Sing thy redeeming grace.]

Hymn 3:14.

The song of Simeon, Luke 2. 28; or,
A sight of Christ makes death easy.

1 Now have our hearts embrac'd our God,
We would forget all earthly charms,
And wish to die as Simeon would,
With his young Saviour in his arms.

2 Our lips should learn that joyful song,
Were but our hearts prepar'd like his;
Our souls still willing to be gone,
And at thy word depart in peace.

3 Here we have seen thy face, O Lord,
And view'd salvation with our eyes,
Tasted and felt the living word,
The bread descending from the skies.

4 Thou hast prepar'd this dying Lamb,
Hast set his blood before our face,
To teach the terrors of thy Name,
And show the wonders of thy grace.

5 He is our light; our morning star
Shall shine on nations yet unknown;

The glory of thine Israel here,
And joy of spirits near the throne.

Hymn 3:15.

Our Lord Jesus at his own table.

1 [The memory of our dying Lord
Awakes a thankful tongue:
How rich he spread his royal board,
And blest the food, and sung.

2 Happy the men that eat this bread,
But double bless'd was he
That gently bow'd his loving head,
And lean'd it, Lord, on thee.

3 By faith the same delights we
taste
As that great favourite did,
And sit and lean on Jesus' breast,
And take the heavenly bread.]

4 Down from the palace of the skies,
Hither the King descends;
"Come my beloved, eat, (he cries)
"And drink salvation, friends.

5 “[My flesh is food and physic too,
“A balm for all your pains;
“And the red streams of pardon flow
“From these my pierced veins.”]

6 Hosanna to his bounteous love
For such a taste below!
And yet he feeds his saints above
With nobler blessings too.

7 [Come the dear day, the glorious hour
That brings our souls to rest!
Then we shall need these types no
more,
But dwell at th’ heavenly feast.]

Hymn 3:16.

The agonies of Christ.

1 Now let our pains be all forgot,
Our hearts no more repine,
Our sufferings are not worth a
thought,
When, Lord, compar’d with thine.

2 In lively figures here we see
The bleeding Prince of love;

Each of us hope he dy'd for me,
And then our griefs remove.

3 [Our humble faith here takes her rise,
While sitting round his board;
And back to Calvary she flies,
To view her groaning Lord.

4 His soul, what agonies it felt
When his own God withdrew!
And the large load of all our guilt
Lay heavy on him too.

5 But the divinity within
Supported him to bear:
Dying he conquer'd hell and sin,
And made his triumph there.]

6 Grace, wisdom, justice join'd and wrought
The wonders of that day:
No mortal tongue, nor mortal thought
Can equal thanks repay.

7 Our hymns should sound like those above,
Could we our voices raise;

Yet, Lord, our hearts shall all be love,
And all our lives be praise.

Hymn 3:17.

Incomparable food; or, The flesh and blood of Christ.

1 [We sing th' amazing deeds
That grace divine performs;
Th' eternal God comes down and
bleeds
To nourish dying worms.

2 This soul reviving wine,
Dear Saviour, 'Tis thy blood;
We thank that sacred flesh of thine
For this immortal food.]

3 The banquet that we eat
Is made of heavenly things,
Earth hath no dainties half so sweet
As our Redeemer brings.

4 In vain had Adam sought
And search'd his garden round,
For there was no such blessed fruit
In all the happy ground.

5 Th' angelic host above
Can never taste this food,
They feast upon their Maker's love,
But not a Saviour's blood.

6 On us th' Almighty Lord
Bestows this matchless grace,
And meets us with some cheering word,
With pleasure in his face.

7 Come, all ye drooping saints,
And banquet with the King,
This wine will drown your sad complaints,
And tune your voice to sing.

8 Salvation to the Name
Of our adored Christ:
Thro' the wide earth his grace proclaim
His glory in the high'st.

Hymn 3:18.

The same.

1 Jesus, we bow before thy feet,
Thy table is divinely stor'd:

Thy sacred flesh our souls have eat,
'Tis living bread; we thank thee, Lord!

2 And here we drink our Saviour's blood,
We thank thee, Lord, 'Tis generous wine;
Mingled with love the fountain flow'd
From that dear bleeding heart of thine.

3 On earth is no such sweetness found,
For the Lamb's flesh is heavenly food;
In vain we search the globe around
For bread so fine, or wine so good.

4 Carnal provisions can at best
But cheer the heart, or warm the head,
But the rich cordial that we taste
Gives life eternal to the dead.

5 Joy to the Master of the feast,
His name our souls for ever bless:
To God the King, and God the Priest,
A loud Hosanna round the place.

Hymn 3:19.

Glory in the cross; or, Not ashamed of Christ crucified.

1 At thy command, our dearest Lord,
Here we attend thy dying feast;
Thy blood like wine adorns thy board,
And thine own flesh feeds every guest.

2 Our faith adores thy bleeding love,
And trusts for life in one that dy'd;
We hope for heavenly crowns above
From a Redeemer crucify'd.

3 Let the vain world pronounce it shame,
And fling their scandals on thy cause;
We come to boast our Saviour's Name,
And make our triumphs in his cross.

4 With joy we tell the scoffing age
He that was dead has left his tomb,
He lives above their utmost rage,
And we are waiting till he come.

Hymn 3:20.

The provisions for the table of our Lord; or, The tree of life, and river of love.

1 Lord, we adore thy bounteous hand,
And sing the solemn feast
Where sweet celestial dainties stand
For every willing guest.

2 [The tree of life adorns the board
With rich immortal fruit,
And ne'er an angry flaming sword
To guard the passage to't.

3 The cup stands crown'd with living juice;
The fountain flows above,
And runs down streaming for our use
In rivulets of love.]

4 The food's prepar'd by heavenly art,
The pleasure's well refin'd,
They spread new life thro' every heart,
And cheer the drooping mind.

5 Shout and proclaim the Saviour's love,
Ye saints that taste his wine,

Join with your kindred saints above,
In loud hosannas join.

6 A thousand glories to the God
That gives such joy as this;
Hosanna! let it sound abroad,
And reach where Jesus is.

Hymn 3:21.

The triumphal feast for Christ's victory over sin, and death, and hell.

1 [Come let us lift our voices high,
High as our joys arise,
And join the songs above the sky,
Where pleasure never dies.

2 Jesus, the God that fought and bled,
And conquer'd when he fell;
That rose, and at his chariot-wheels
Dragg'd all the powers of hell.]

3 [Jesus the God invites us here
To this triumphal feast,
And brings immortal blessings down
For each redeemed guest.]

4 The Lord! how glorious is his face!
How kind his smiles appear!
And O what melting words he says
To every humble ear!

5 "For you, the children of my love,
"It was for you I dy'd;
"Behold my hands, behold my feet,
"And look into my side.

6 "These are the wounds for you I bore,
"The tokens of my pains,
"When I came down to free your souls
"From misery and chains.

7 "Justice unsheath'd its fiery sword,
And plung'd it in my heart;
"Infinite pangs for you I bore,
"And most tormenting smart.

8 "When hell and all its spiteful powers
"Stood dreadful in my way,
"To rescue those dear lives of yours
"I gave my own away.

9 "But while I bled, and groan'd, and dy'd,
"I ruin'd Satan's throne;
"High on my cross I hung, and spy'd
"The monster tumbling down.

10 "Now you must triumph at my feast,
"And taste my flesh, my blood;
"And live eternal ages bless'd,
"For 'Tis immortal food."

11 Victorious God! what can we pay
For favours so divine?
We would devote our hearts away
To be for ever thine.

12 We give thee, Lord, our highest praise,
The tribute of our tongues;
But themes so infinite as these
Exceed our noblest songs.

Hymn 3:22.

The compassion of a dying Christ.

1 Our spirits join t' adore the Lamb;
O that our feeble lips could move
In strains immortal as his Name,
And melting as his dying love.

2 Was ever equal pity found?
The Prince of heaven resigns his breath,

And pours his life out on the ground
To ransom guilty worms from death.

3 [Rebels, we broke our Maker's laws;
He from the threatening set us free,
Bore the full vengeance on his cross,
And nail'd the curses to the tree.]

4 [The law proclaims no terror now,
And Sinai's thunder roars no more;
From all his wounds new blessings flow,
A sea of joy without a shore.

5 Here we have wash'd our deepest stains,
And heal'd our wounds with heavenly blood:
Bless'd fountain! springing from the veins
Of Jesus, our incarnate God.]

6 In vain our mortal voices strive
To speak compassion so divine;
Had we a thousand lives to give,
A thousand lives should all be thine.

Hymn 3:23.

Grace and glory by the death of Christ.

1 [Sitting around our Father's board
We raise our tuneful breath;
Our faith beholds her dying Lord,
And dooms our sins to death.]

2 We see the blood of Jesus shed,
Whence all our pardons rise;
The sinner views th' atonement made,
And loves the sacrifice.

3 Thy cruel thorns, thy shameful cross
Procure us heavenly crowns;
Our highest gain springs from thy loss,
Our healing from thy wounds.

4 O 'tis impossible that we,
Who dwell in feeble clay,
Should equal sufferings bear for thee,
Or equal thanks repay.

Hymn 3:24.

Pardon and strength from Christ.

1 Father, we wait to feel thy grace,
To see thy glories shine;
The Lord will his own table bless,
And make the feast divine.

2 We touch, we taste the heavenly bread,
We drink the sacred Cup;
With outward forms our sense is fed,
Our souls rejoice in hope.

3 We shall appear before the throne
Of our forgiving God,
Dress'd in the garments of his Son,
And sprinkled with his blood.

4 We shall be strong to run the race,
And climb the upper sky;
Christ will provide our souls with grace,
He bought a large supply.

5 [Let us indulge a cheerful frame,
For joy becomes a feast;
We love the memory of his Name,
More than the wine we taste.]

Hymn 3:25.

Divine glories, and our graces.

1 How are thy glories here display'd,
Great God, how bright they shine,
While at thy word we break the
bread,
And pour the flowing wine!

2 Here thy revenging justice stands
And pleads its dreadful cause;
Here saving mercy spreads her
hands
Like Jesus on the cross.

3 Thy saints attend with every grace
On this great sacrifice;
And love appears with cheerful face,
And faith with fixed eyes.

4 Our hope in waiting posture sits,
To heaven directs her sight;
Here every warmer passion meets,
And warmer powers unite.

5 Zeal and revenge perform their part,
And rising sin destroy;

Repentance comes with aching
heart,
Yet not forbids the joy.

6 Dear Saviour, change our faith to sight,
Let sin for ever die;
Then shall our souls be all delight,
And every tear be dry.

* * * * * *

I cannot persuade myself to put a full period to these Divine Hymns, till I have addressed a special song of glory to God the Father, the Son, and the Holy Spirit. Though the Latin name of it, Gloria Patri, be retained in our nation from the Romish church; and thought there may be some excesses of superstitious honour paid to the words of it, which may have wrought some unhappy prejudices in weaker Christians, yet I believe it still to be one of the noblest parts of Christian worship. The subject of it is the doctrine of the Trinity, which is that peculiar glory of the Divine Nature, that our Lord Jesus Christ has so clearly revealed unto men, and is so necessary to true Christianity.

The action is praise, which is one of the most complete and exalted parts of heavenly worship. I have cast the song into a variety of forms, and have fitted it to a plain version, or a larger paraphrase, to be sung either alone, or at the conclusion of another Hymn. I have added also a few hosannas, or ascriptions of salvation to Christ, in the same manner, and for the same end.

Doxologies

Hymn 3:26. 1st. L.M.

A song of praise to the ever-blessed Trinity, God in Father, Son, and Spirit.

1 Bless'd be the Father and his love:
To whose celestial source we owe
Rivers of endless joy above,
And rills of comfort here below.

2 Glory to thee, great Son of God,
From whose dear wounded body rolls
A precious stream of vital blood,
Pardon and life for dying souls.

3 We give the sacred Spirit praise,
Who in our hearts of sin and woe
Makes living springs of grace arise,
And into boundless glory flow.

4 Thus God the Father, God the Son,
And God the Spirit, we adore;
That sea of life and love unknown,
Without a bottom or a shore.

Hymn 3:27. 1st. C. M.

1 Glory to God the Father's Name,
Who, from our sinful race,
Chose out his favourites to proclaim
The honours of his grace.

2 Glory to God the Son be paid,
Who dwelt in humble clay,
And, to redeem us from the dead,
Gave his own life away.

3 Glory to God the Spirit give,
From whose almighty power
Our souls their heavenly birth derive,
And bless the happy hour.

4 Glory to God that reigns above,
Th' eternal Three and One,
Who by the wonders of his love
Has made his nature known.

Hymn 3:28. 1st. S. M.

1 Let God the Father live
For ever on our tongues;
Sinners from his first love derive
The ground of all their songs.

2 Ye saints, employ your breath
In honour to the Son,
Who bought your souls from hell
and death
By offering up his own.

3 Give to the Spirit praise
Of an immortal strain,
Whose light and power and grace
conveys
Salvation down to men.

4 While God the Comforter
Reveals our pardon'd sin,
O may the blood and water bear
The same record within.

5 To the great One and Three
That seal this grace in heaven,
The Father, Son, and Spirit, be
Eternal glory given.

Hymn 3:29. 2d. L.M.

1 Glory to God the Trinity
Whose name has mysteries unknown;
In essence One, in person Three;
A social nature, yet alone.

2 When all our noblest powers are
join'd
The honours of thy Name to raise,
Thy glories over-match our mind,
And angels faint beneath the praise.

Hymn 3:30. 2d. C. M

1 The God of mercy be ador'd,
Who calls our souls from death,
Who saves by his redeeming word,
And new-creating breath.

2 To praise the Father and the Son
And Spirit all divine,
The One in Three, and Three in One,
Let saints and angels join.

Hymn 3:31. 2d. S. M.

1 Let God the Maker's name
Have honour, love and fear,
To God the Saviour pay the same,
And God the Comforter.

2 Father of lights above,
Thy mercy we adore,

The Son of thy eternal love
And Spirit of thy power.

Hymn 3:32. 3d. L. M.

To God the Father, God the Son,
And God the Spirit, Three in One,
Be honour, praise, and glory given,
By all on earth, and all in heaven.

Hymn 3:33.

Or thus:

All glory to thy wondrous Name,
Father of mercy, God of love,
Thus we exalt the Lord, the Lamb,
And thus we praise the heavenly Dove.

Hymn 3:34. 3d. C. M.

Now let the Father and the Son
And Spirit be ador'd,
Where there are works to make him known,
Or saints to love the Lord.

Hymn 3:35.

Or thus:

Honour to thee, almighty Three,
And everlasting One;
All glory to the Father be,
The Spirit, and the Son.

Hymn 3:36. 3d. S. M.

Ye angels round the throne
And saints that dwell below,
Worship the Father, love the Son,
And bless the Spirit too.

Hymn 3:37.

Or thus:

Give to the Father praise,
Give glory to the Son,
And to the Spirit of his grace
Be equal honour done.

Hymn 3:38.

A song of praise to the blessed Trinity.

The 1st, as the 148th Psalm.

1 I give immortal praise
To God the Father's love
For all my comforts here,
And better hopes above;
He sent his own
Eternal Son,
To die for sins
That man had done.

2 To God the Son belongs
Immortal glory too,
Who bought us with his
  blood
From everlasting woe;
And now he lives,
And now he reigns,
And sees the fruit
Of all his pains.

3 To God the Spirit's Name
Immortal worship give,
Whose new-creating power

Makes the dead sinner live:
His work completes
The great design
And fills the soul
With joy divine.

4 Almighty God, to thee
Be endless honours done,
The undivided Three,
And the mysterious one:
Where reason fails
With all her powers,
There faith prevails,
And love adores.

Hymn 3:39.

The 2d, as the 148th Psalm.

1 To Him that chose us first
Before the world began,
To Him that bore the curse
To save rebellious man,
To Him that form'd
Our hearts anew,
Is endless praise
And glory due.

2 The Father's love shall run
Thro' our immortal songs,
We bring to God the Son
Hosannas on our tongues:
Our lips address
The Spirit's Name
With equal praise,
And zeal the same.

3 Let every saint above
And angel round the throne,
For ever bless and love
The sacred Three in One:
Thus heaven shall raise
His honours high
When earth and time
Grow old and die.

Hymn 3:40.

The 3d, as the 148th Psalm.

To God the Father's throne
Perpetual honours raise;
Glory to God the Son,
To God the Spirit praise:
And while our lips
Their tribute bring,

Our faith adores
The name we sing.

Hymn 3:41.

Or thus:

To our eternal God,
The Father and the Son,
And Spirit all divine,
Three mysteries in one,
Salvation, power,
And praise be given
By all on earth
And all in heaven.

Hymn 3:42. L. M.

The Hosanna; or, Salvation ascribed to Christ.

1 Hosanna to King David's Son,
Who reigns on a superior throne;
We bless the Prince of heavenly
birth
Who brings salvation down to
earth.

2 Let every nation, every age,
In this delightful work engage;
Old men and babes in Sion sing
The growing glories of her King.

Hymn 3:43. C. M.

1 Hosanna to the Prince of Grace,
Sion, behold her King;
Proclaim the Son of David's race,
And teach the babes to sing.

2 Hosanna to th' incarnate Word,
Who from the Father came;
Ascribe salvation to the Lord,
With blessings on his Name.

Hymn 3:44. S. M.

1 Hosanna to the Son
Of David and of God,
Who brought the news of pardon
down,
And bought it with his blood,

2 To Christ th' anointed King
Be endless blessings given,

Let the whole earth his glory sing
Who made our peace with heaven.

Hymn 3:45. As the 148th Psalm.

1 Hosanna to the King
Of David's ancient blood;
Behold he comes to bring
Forgiving grace from God:
Let old and young
Attend his way,
And at his feet
Their honours lay.

2 Glory to God on high,
Salvation to the Lamb;
Let earth, and sea, and sky
His wondrous love proclaim:
Upon his head
Shall honours rest,
And every age
Pronounce him blest.

THE END.

Printed in the United States
111988LV00001B/15/A

9 788189 952730